Ezio Manzini

LIVABLE PROXIMITY

Ideas for the City that Cares

With a Contribution by
Ivana Pais

Translation: Andrew Spannaus and Anne Kendall for Language Solutions for Business - London
Cover: Cristina Bernasconi, Milan
Typesetting: Laura Panigara, Cesano Boscone (MI)

EGEA S.p.A.
Via Salasco, 5 - 20136 Milano
Tel. 02/5836.5751 – Fax 02/5836.5753
egea.edizioni@unibocconi.it – www.egeaeditore.it

First edition: February 2022

ISBN Domestic Edition	978-88-99902-87-2
ISBN International Edition	978-88-31322-38-6
ISBN Digital Domestic Edition	978-88-238-8381-9
ISBN Digital International Edition	978-88-31322-56-0

Print: Logo s.r.l., Borgoricco (PD)

"*Livable Proximity* is a passionate and compelling call for a remaking of the city under a novel paradigm of relationality and care by one of the most accomplished design thinkers of our time. Manzini lucidly demonstrates why a novel practice of urban dwelling based on proximity is not only desirable and possible but essential for a functional, place-based, and Earth-wise human sociality. In Manzini's skillful hands, 'proximity' emerges as a trope for a complex spatial, social, and cultural imagination of the city that challenges head on the increasingly individualizing and isolating tendencies of post-pandemic living. While anchored in enlightening analyses of Barcelona, Milano, and Paris, Manzini's visionary architecture of proximity should serve as a guide for urban professionals and citizens worldwide wishing to counter the de-localizing and de-communalizing effects of the modernist 'city of distance'. This eminently readable book will be of great value to urban planners and designers and to geography, anthropology, and urban ecology scholars, as well as to the growing cadre of citizens' groups concerned with urban futures."

– **Arturo Escobar**, Professor of Anthropology Emeritus, University of North Carolina, Chapel Hill; author of *Designs for the Pluriverse: Radical Interdependence, Autonomy, and the Making of Worlds*

"Proximity only makes sense if it serves to share within the community. The new urbanism must learn from social innovation to design affective, effective and healing neighborhoods. Once again, Manzini opens our eyes to real possibilities for positive change in society through innovative and humanistic design. A must read for urban planners and mayors."

– **Juli Capella**, architect and designer; former President of FAD (Promotion of Architecture and Design); member of Advisory Council of Superilla for Barcelona City Council

"With deep reflection and insightful wisdom Ezio Manzini draws us into *Livable Proximity*. This book is an excellent perspective on how to think about places and communities that care, I commend it to everyone who does indeed care about cities."

– **Rachel Cooper**, PhD OBE, Distinguished Professor of Design Policy, Lancaster University

"Covid-19 is still raging around the world. It will have a decisive impact on the future way of life of all humankind. Among the many important challenges and opportunities accompanying these changes is the re-discovery of the lost intrinsic value of residential community. *Livable Proximity* – the new book by Professor Ezio Manzini – explores the potential methods and possible scenarios for reviving and further developing the legacy of the precious proximity of urban life, given this new era characterized by digitization and sustainable development. This is also the latest and most concrete version of the SLOC (Small, Local, Open, and Connected) paradigm that Professor Manzini has advocated for many years."

– **Yongqi Lou**, Vice President & Dean of the College of Design and Innovation, Tongji University

"Trying to determine the direction of design – while observing human society from the perspective written in this book – I can feel a tactile nostalgic future."

– **Fumikazu Masuda**, designer; founder of open house inc.

"Manzini redefines proximity for the digital age, revealing a delightful, creative, sociable way of living. New, yet familiar, merging tradition with technology. Feasible. Already in place in cities large and small across the world yielding communities where attention is focused upon social dimensions of interaction, not upon technology. A powerful, important way to live sustainably in the 21st century."

– **Don Norman**, Professor emeritus, The Design Lab, University of California, San Diego; author of *Design of Everyday Things*

"This thoughtful reflection on cities of the future is a useful tonic to the feeling of uncertainty that dominates our lives today. A must read for anyone pondering the way we live in harmony with people and the planet."

– **Louise Pulford**, CEO of SIX, Social Innovation Exchange

"Is the digital world inexorably controlled by the internet giants of Silicon Valley? What an error! This book demonstrates how proximity and digitalization profit from each other. Projects like the ‹15-minute city›, sharing economy, collaborative care, fab-labs, distributed energy production, civic agriculture, are unthinkable without digital tools. Technology from the grassroots perspective!"

– **Wolfgang Sachs**, Senior Researcher, Wuppertal Institute for Climate, Environment, Energy, Berlin Office; editor of *The Development Dictionary. A Guide to Knowledge as Power*; author of *Planet Dialectics. Explorations in Environment and Development*

"The prospect of a city that cares brings new meaning and vitality to places exhausted by a focus on capital, concrete, and consumption. In these inspirational pages, the word local is brought back to life by the pre-eminent social designer of our time. Ezio Manzini reveals a design practice which enhances the social, spatial and relational qualities of the places where we live."

– **John Thackara**, author of *How to Thrive in the Next Economy*

"Making social and environmental sustainability compatible are the two great challenges of our time. And there is a common link between the two that Professor Manzini's book discovers and highlights: proximity. And it shows us a playground where, with advanced social experiments, cities try to meet these challenges through innovation."

– **Lluís Torrens**, Director of Social Innovation, Barcelona City Council

"The author's passionate subject shines on the life of the city in which he masterfully combines his vision with his approach on design for social innovation, which he pioneered two decades ago. He dances a journey with his full knowledge and expertise on the theme of livable cities: the architectural and molecular view, technological and social design, particularly strategic design for sustainability. All dimensions of city and proximity are explored in width and depth with warmth, full of empathy and validation at the same time. Thus, the book is not for urban experts only but for people who are interested and concerned with the city and its well-being too."

– **Wallapa van Willenswaard**, co-founder of INI-Innovation Network International; Head of Team, School for Wellbeing Studies and Research, Thailand

"This book is not only at the edge of knowledge about social innovation. It's above all a set of inspiring ideas for all those who want to rebuild our communities after the Covid-19 pandemic and to make our future ecological and social contract a reality."

– Stéphane Vincent, délégué général, La 27e Région

Table of Contents

Introduction 1

1 Trajectories of Proximity 9
  1.1 What is proximity? 10
    Box 1.1 Dimensions of proximity 10
  1.2 Functional proximity and relational proximity 11
    Box 1.2 Project-based communities 12
  1.3 Diversified proximity and specialized proximity 14
  1.4 Technical innovation and hybrid proximity 16
    Box 1.3 Distributed systems 17
  1.5 Social innovation and relational proximity 19
    Box 1.4 Social Innovation 19
  1.6 Cultural innovation and more-than-human proximity 21
    Box 1.5 Systems of proximity and the web of life 22
  1.7 Livable proximity 23

2 The City of Proximity 27
  2.1 The city of common goods 27
    Box 2.1 Common goods and community 29
  2.2 The city of distances and its crisis 31
  2.3 Competing scenarios 32
  2.4 Everything in less than 15 minutes, but not only 33
    Example 1 *Paris and the 15-minute city* 34
  2.5 Functional proximity and "minimum ecological units" 37
    Example 2 *Barcelona and the superilles* 38

2.6   Relational proximity, local networks, and cosmopolitism   40

     Box 2.2   Cosmopolitan localism   42

2.7   The double link between functional and relational proximity   44

2.8   Encounters, meeting places, and the molecular dimension
of the city   46

     Box 2.3   Anti-epidemic proxemics   48

2.9   Local communities, diversified proximity, and resilience   49

2.10   Streets, squares, common goods, and proximity   51

     Box 2.4   Remote work as a regenerative agent
by *Ivana Pais*   52

3   The City that Cares   **59**

3.1   Care and proximity / Care is proximity   60

     Box 3.1   Being in contact without contact   62

3.2   Care is also care work   63

     Box 3.2   The nature of care work   66

3.3   Careless cities   67

3.4   Services that help collaborate   70

     Box 3.3   Capabilities and enabling systems   74

3.5   Communities of care   75

     Example 3   *The circle model for the construction of communities*   76

3.6   Proximity that cares   80

     Example 4   *Social Superilles and localization of services*   81

3.7   Care, communities, and hybrid proximities   84

     Example 5   *Radars: a network of human sensors*   86

     Example 6   *WeMi: a platform and many hybrid places*   87

3.8   Redistributing care work   89

3.9   A new ecology of time   91

3.10   Density and economies of proximity   92

4   Designing to Bring Close   **99**

4.1   Technical and social infrastructure as platforms
of opportunity   100

4.2   From the city of distances to the city of proximity   103

4.3   Stimuli and attractors of the social conversation   107

4.4   Communities of place as an interweave of projects   110

     Example 7   *North of Loreto, a neighborhood as a project-based
incubator,* by *Davide Fassi*   110

4.5   Construction and regeneration   116

     Example 8 *Collaborative living at maturity: the experience of the social housing foundation in Milan*, by *Giordana Ferri*   117

4.6   From the heroic phase to transformative normality   122

4.7   Designing in proximity and for proximity   126

4.8   Community, proximity, projects   128

     Box 4.1 Designing in complexity   130

Proximate Future.
Cities of Proximity and Digital Platforms, by *Ivana Pais*   135

Defining the concept of digital platform   136

Platforms of livable proximity and questions of governance   139

  The new municipalism   142

The relational (but not only) dimension of digital platforms   143

  The sharing economy   144

Urban platforms and local roots   148

  Sharing cities   151

Proximate future: platforms as new "local collective goods"?   154

Introduction

1. This book is a contribution to the social conversation on cities and their future.

The book revives an idea that has been circulating for some time, and that in recent years has received greater attention: that of a city of proximity, in which everything that people need for daily life is just a few minutes away by foot from where they live. This is also a city in which functional proximity corresponds to relational proximity, thanks to which people have more opportunities to see each other, support each other, take care of both each other and the environment, and collaborate to reach goals together. Ultimately, it is a city constructed on the life of its citizens, and on an idea of *livable proximity* in which people can find everything they need to live, and to do so together with others.

This city of proximity, or the "15-minute city" as it is now often called, proposes a clear and simple vision of the direction to be taken, giving strength to the idea. But implementing this vision requires a deep cultural change and strong political will: it is necessary to definitively break with a vision of a city divided into specialized parts, and as a consequence, to carry out a radical reorganization of existing infrastructure and forms of governance. Above all, it requires combatting the inequalities that characterize society, and thus contemporary cities as well. The advantage of proximity cannot merely be the prerogative of some privileged neighborhoods, but must extend to the entire city. It must be a right for all citizens.

The underlying issue posed by the book is this: can we construct the contemporary city starting from a new idea of proximity? The response that the book gives is yes, it can be done. And, I add, the social innovations of the last twenty years give us a concrete indication of how to do so; or at least where to start.

Recent history shows us that, in numerous ways and on various themes, these innovations can generate forms of community and proximity that go in the direction indicated here: communities linked to things to do together and places in which to do them; open and dynamic systems of proximity in which these initiatives are situated, that at the same time collaborate for regeneration of the communities; hybrid proximities, whose existence largely depends on the digital instruments at their disposal.

On the other hand, if these initiatives give concrete form to the proposal of the city of proximity, the relationship between social innovation and proximity could also be read in the opposite direction: the city of proximity could become the common horizon for the many different types of experimentation that have taken place in recent years. Thus, it could give cities more strength and more possibilities to spread.

2. The theme of cities of proximity, in its essence, is not new: it can be observed that there are cities, or more often parts of cities, that already approach this condition (having inherited neighborhoods from the pre-modern past in which the limits of public transportation meant that all daily life had to be based on proximity). Moreover, this theme has returned to circulation with different names and, driven by environmental motivations (reduction of traffic, and thus of pollution) and social motivations (the fight against solitude and for quality of life), some cities have launched projects and programs based on this idea.

Given this, it is urgent today to revive the discussion of the theme in light of what has happened in the last twenty years, and is happening today. The backdrop is the growing evidence of the interaction between environmental crisis, with the need to question the ways and times in which this crisis must be addressed, and the social crisis given by the increase of the distance between those who accumulate wealth and those who have less and less, with the need to regenerate the urban fabric.

In this context of difficulty the pandemic then exploded, with all of the dramatic implications we are experiencing. Even though we are not yet able to predict the full consequences of this event, the book shows some aspects that are already sufficiently clear. We can in fact see that everywhere, the pandemic has reignited the discussion on the future of cities and more in general on the physical and territorial dimensions of sociotechnical systems. And that is not all. It is certain that the pandemic has produced changes in behavior on a scale and of a depth that would have been unimaginable beforehand. One of the most evident is the movement of the center of gravity of productive activities and consumption towards the digital dimension, with growing portions of work, studies, and entertainment online, and with all of the relevant implications in terms of daily mobility, social relations, and the use of cities and their services.

Faced with these phenomena, the idea of the city of proximity seems to be extraordinarily relevant today: it can in fact be a positive and workable guideline for environmental and social challenges, as they had been posed well before the pandemic. But it could also be the best proposal for the post-pandemic society, and in particular to oppose the emerging city of "everything at/from home": de facto a non-city of self-confined individuals in isolation in their homes, who for reasons of convenience, could continue to live this way even when it is no longer an obligation. Ultimately, the city of proximity, in which everything is close by, can be the perspective that allows for combatting this dystopian, but unfortunately very powerful and already widely operational condition of everything at/from home.

3. Therefore, the issue is not new: much has already been said and many are discussing it. What does this book add to the debate? Its minimum goal is to contribute to articulating and examining the theme of proximity in depth, showing how it touches various aspects and different dimensions of cities and the experience of citizens within them. Set against this basic motivation, there are then more ambitious aims, which can be summarized in three points.

The first concerns the *construction of communities*. Many authors and writings converge on the idea that, given the multiple crises we are facing, it is necessary to re-establish the social fabric and (re)construct communities.

But once this goal has been set, the next step is usually missing, which is both simple to state but difficult to achieve: how do we (re)construct a community? And when a community already exists, how do we help it regenerate itself and last in time? The book tries to give a response, which briefly, is as follows: a community cannot be designed because it is a social form that emerges from multiple events. What can be done is to create a suitable environment, and if necessary, produce stimulus that generates encounters and launches conversations from which new communities can emerge. Here the question of proximity comes into play: experience shows that communities need an environment in which there is appropriate proximity; that is, a system of proximity that is sufficiently diversified and balanced between its functional and relational components. Certainly, there is no guarantee that, given these conditions, communities will truly be formed. But we can say with the same level of certainty that these favorable conditions, that we call the city of proximity, make the birth and life of new communities more likely. So returning to the initial question, in concrete terms, these favorable conditions are what must be designed.

The second point is linked to the first one and to how to design a city of proximity focusing on the *relationship between cities, proximity, and care*. Recently, there has been much discussion about care, intended as care work and also other modes of interaction between human beings, and in general, between human beings and everything that makes up the network of life. There has been much discussion on how and why the city of services, as it has existed until now, is a careless city; a city in which the inhabitants are no longer seen as citizens capable of care, but only as (potential) users and clients of services. The book considers these discussions and advances the hypothesis that to regenerate a city capable of care, it is necessary to develop new communities; and that to do so, a new generation of services is *also* necessary: collaborative services, distributed throughout the local territory, that can represent a stimulus and supporting infrastructure for these new communities. The observation of social innovation tells us that this can be done by operating simultaneously on multiple levels: bringing services and activities close to citizens (*localization*), favoring the construction of communities (*socialization*); extending the network of actors involved (*inclusion*); involving actors initially not considered (*diversification*); and horizontally connecting different areas of intervention (*coordination*).

The third point concerns *the relationship between the physical and digital dimensions of proximity*. For some time now there has been discussion of the increasingly hybrid, physical-digital character of the space in which we act and how the great social experiment imposed by the pandemic has accelerated this process. The book assumes that today we cannot speak of proximity, community, and care without taking this factor into account. Proximity, community, and care, despite being rooted in the physical world, have an increasingly important digital component, and could no longer exist without it. On the other hand, this digital component, that today is largely represented by the different forms of platforms, is not neutral. Each platform supports activities but has characteristics that, de facto, orient the activities that it makes possible. This is why platforms must be designed with a clear idea of the type of activity intended to be promoted and supported, and thus the social forms one wishes to see emerge. These themes are further examined in the essay by Ivana Pais that concludes the book.

4. The city is a complex organism. To speak of it we must adopt different points of view, including views showing it from above, as a whole, and a view from the inside. The book adopts the second of these, which is the view of the citizens. This perspective from the inside is also indispensable if we truly want to speak of proximity and care.

On the other hand, since everything that we can say on these questions depends on the context to which we refer, to speak about the subject I had to make some choices. And I chose cases situated in the contexts I knew the best, principally Milan and Barcelona. In both of these cities much has been done on the theme discussed here. But I certainly could have found good examples elsewhere as well: from Turin to Copenhagen, to remain within the classic typology of European cities; or from New York to Shanghai or Seoul, to open up to other urban forms and histories; or I could have spoken of the density and proximity of the favelas in Rio or the slums of Nairobi. Each city would have had its own story to tell, but I would not have had enough direct experiences to do this, so I leave this task to others.

However, once the inevitable specificity of each case has been recognized, along with the limits of what it can tell others in other contexts, I believe that, if we know how to recognize and interpret them, each case has something to teach everyone, applicable to every context. Referring to European cities to discuss proximity can certainly be seen as the easiest choice: if compared with cities with high vertical density (cities of skyscrapers) or those with low density (cities of suburbs) or informal cities (cities of slums and favelas), European cities seem intrinsically closer to the proposal of a city of proximity. Thus focusing on them as cases of reference means making the easiest choice. This is true. If, however, it is necessary to break a consolidated cultural and operational model such as that of the city of distances, and at the same time divert the tendency underway towards non-cities of everything at/from home, this seems to be the most reasonable choice: if the task is difficult, then it is useful to start from a place that is (relatively) easy. Moreover, while it is true that in the cities to which we refer there are (still) some neighborhoods rich with activities and services of proximity, this quality has been under attack for years, and it is necessary to do something to invert the processes of social desertification underway and trigger the evolution of what remains of pre-modern proximity, that still characterizes them, towards contemporary forms of proximity. That is not all: while it is true that in some historical neighborhoods of these cities the system of proximity is sufficiently diversified and relational, there are others in which this is not the case at all. In these same cities, the challenge is thus to extend the idea of the city of proximity to the entire urban territory, including the parts in which this appears most difficult.

5. The book is divided into four chapters, plus a substantial final essay by Ivana Pais.

The first chapter introduces the other three, discussing the theme of proximity, considering its different meanings and the dynamics of its current evolution. The second speaks of the city and its evolution considering it from the standpoint of the forms of proximity that can be found in it: the city as a mixture of systems of proximity. Three scenarios are introduced: the *city of distances*, as a scenario of the cities that the previous century produced and passed down to us, and two new scenarios that are currently competing, that of the *city of everything at/from home*, and that of the *city of proximity*. The third chapter discusses the relationship between cities, proximity, and care, considering the latter as a form of interaction – between people and between people and the world – on which the construction of cities of proximity should be based. The book assumes that what is called the city of services has become the city without care, and attributes this result to how services themselves have been conceived and carried out. Starting from this point, it indicates two complementary strategies to contribute to constructing the city of proximity as a city of care. The fourth chapter zooms in on the heart of all of the previous proposals, i.e. if and how it is possible to design new communities that can act as the basis for all possible cities of proximity and care. The close observation of two cases allows for recognizing the weave of designs, of different natures and scales, of which these communities consist and on which they feed to last over time. Starting from those cases, the book discusses in more general terms the implications in terms of design strategies.

The concluding essay by Ivana Pais introduces and discusses the theme of digital platforms for cities, showing their complex nature, evolution in time, and the contribution that, if correctly designed, they could make to the city of proximity.

6. The contents of this book are the results of many stories that came together before and during the writing process: that of the author and the experiences on the theme of design for city-making in recent years in many cities of the world, and in particular, in Barcelona and Milan; that of Ivana Pais, with whom the idea for the book was born during a conversation in a bar in October 2020; that of Giordana Ferri, with whom I discussed the theme of living proximity and with whom, in November 2020, I organized an initiative of the same name; that of Davide Fassi, who very generously introduced me to one of the cases that was most useful to bring the ideas proposed in this book into focus; those of Lekshmy Parameswaran and Julia Benini, with whom we organized an event on communities of care; and those of Hilary Cottam and Lluis Torrens, who helped fill it with content. Lastly, there is the encounter with Albert Fuster, Roger Paez, and many other colleagues at Elisava, with whom I worked for three years in Barcelona on the issue of design for cities.

A book is also its cover image, which in this case came from a talk with my son Matteo, who gave us the gift of a contemporary interpretation of the *Allegory of Good Government*: the great fresco in the *Palazzo Pubblico* of Siena in which, seven hundred years ago, Ambrogio Lorenzetti depicted much of which should be done today, to which this book intends to contribute.

Finally, a book is a book. It is a product, the result of the work of a group of people who decide to invest in an idea and help it become an actual book. In this regard I thank Alessia Uslenghi, Cinzia Facchi and Cristina Casati of Egea for the trust, flexibility, and professional contribution they made to the success of this project.

1 Trajectories of Proximity

The proximity we will speak of here is the condition of being physically close in space.

But it is also the feeling deriving from the consciousness of sharing something with someone.

This concept, with both of its meanings, seems particularly important to us. For a long time, the issue on the agenda has been: how to make things work despite being far away, farther and farther away. Now we have to pose the opposite problem: how to make things work being close, as close as possible; how to make things work in proximity.

There are good reasons to do this. We have in fact discovered that it is not possible to face problems on the largest scale without starting from what is around us, from the system of proximity of which we are a part. Environmental, social, and economic crises are certainly the result of long chains of interactions, that can also extend a long way. But when they begin to touch our experience and our action, they do so in a system of proximity; that is, in the physical space where we are located, and in which each of us constructs our own ideas.

The concept of proximity is certainly ambiguous. If we say that proximity is the quality of a system whose elements can easily enter into direct contact, what exactly do we mean with this expression? What do we mean by "physically close"? There is no precise answer: each person, or perhaps each social group, can give a response in terms of distance to travel or time to arrive. Despite this, at any moment, for each social group, an idea of proximity exists, and there are activities that are considered as practices of proximity. Moreover, since the term has been recognized as important in various disciplines, the words have been found to discuss it, to debate and construct common practices.

1.1   What is proximity?

If the proximity we speak of is the condition of being physically close in space, who and what are the entities whose closeness we wish to discuss? And then: in what sense should this proximity be considered? That is, what does it mean to be proximate?

Proximity is a quality referring to a system whose nodes are entities that interact while physically close, that we will call a *system of proximity*. In turn, this is a subsystem of a broader system that extends well beyond what is close to us, that is part of a network of interactions that includes not only human beings and the products of human activities, but also everything living and non-living around us. To speak of it, though, we must decide the point of view to adopt, and have the right words to do so.

There are in fact many ways to speak of proximity. The commonly-used term has been adopted and defined by many disciplines: from social psychology to economic geography to the study of organizations, passing through economics and Gestalt theory. Each of these gives a different interpretation and identifies different characteristics. Obviously, everyone considers proximity in physical space, but everyone discusses it from their own point of view, and, based on their own interests, indicates what they consider to be the other aspects that distinguish the concept.

Here, we will do it with the intention of discussing what we can – and what we cannot – do in proximity, and how we can do it. Where the "what" we can do has evident operational and functional implications. While the "how" also has qualitative and relational implications, that are less evident but just as important. Let us take a closer look.

Box 1.1   Dimensions of proximity

The characterization of the concept of proximity that is most frequently used, and closest to our interests, is that proposed by Ron Boschma, twenty years ago, in the area of social geography (and it was originally used in the study of the territorial position of organizations). It suggests five dimensions of proximity: geographic, cognitive, social, organizational, and institutional:[1]

- *geographic proximity* is the physical distance between the entities considered. It can be understood as the physical distance between them or the time necessary to go from one to the other;

- *social proximity* refers to the relationships between the entities considered
  and is characterized by mutual trust that, in turn, can depend on kinship,
  friendship, long-term association, or prior experiences;
- *cognitive proximity* is based on closeness in the way of seeing, interpreting,
  understanding, and evaluating the world. It is a closeness necessary to allow
  for communication, the exchange of experiences, and the transfer of knowledge;
- *organizational proximity* indicates what the entities considered have in common in terms of structures and processes both inside of them, and in relation
  to higher-level organizations;
- *institutional proximity* is to be understood as the closeness between the leg-
  islative provisions and administrative requirements in force in a given area
  and the informal system of values and behavioral models characterizing the
  entities considered.

1.2 Functional proximity and relational proximity

The *functional properties* of proximity are those that allow for living and doing what you must do, and want to do. They allow us to act on the world, but before this, they allow us to live, in the biological sense of being alive. It is in proximity that the continuity of what our vital functions require must be guaranteed; which is as important as it is usually little recognized.

Or at least, it is not recognized as it should be: we all clearly see how important for our proximity to include the function of "air conditioning" in a torrid summer; it's harder to recognize that air itself is part of the system of proximity. Or more precisely, it's harder to recognize that purpose when the air is breathable, so we don't think of it. This is only one example, but it reminds us that proximity is where all of the common goods offered by the place in which we are located meet and intersect: air, with its properties we cited, but also all of the physical, animal, and plant world that, from our standpoint, contributes to the livability of a place. This property of systems of proximity, that we tend not to see (taking it for granted), is however clearly the basis not only of the quality of our life, but also of our very existence.

In addition to these properties defined by the nature of the location, proximity has others that depend on a variety of artifacts (buildings, products, services, and communication systems) that by supplementing the former, aim to improve livability. The nature, variety, and number of these artifacts characterize different forms of proximity. So there are different possible ways of living. In other words, our system of proximity includes everything that connects us to the broader sociotechnical systems, together with what connects us to the ecosystem of living and non-living entities of which we ourselves are a part.[2]

As said, the proximity we are discussing cannot be described only with the functions that are performed in it, but must also be considered for how it takes place; that is, for its relational qualities.

The *relational properties* of proximity are those relating to its capacity to generate sociality. In fact, the system of proximity of which we are a part can facilitate or hinder our possibility to meet each other, collaborate, produce shared identities, and ultimately a community. We should briefly explore what this means today.

The relational properties of proximity are obviously less tangible than the functional properties, but not less important. In common language, "being close" refers to a sense of human closeness, i.e. of mutual empathy and trust.[3] For this reason, relational properties also define if and to what extent a given system of proximity can be a favorable environment for the birth, spread, and continuity in time of new forms of community.

The concept of community that we will use must be contextualized and characterized. We are not speaking here of the old pre-modern communities, of villages or neighborhoods, that were communities constructed in historical times whose members were a part of them by birth (because they were born in them). These communities still exist in many parts of the world, but these are not what we refer to. We are speaking of the light, open communities, intentionally built around a project.[4]

Lastly, it is very important whether they refer to a place or not. Since today it is also possible to share interests and projects with people who are physically distant, it is important to consider how and when these communities – and thus these projects of theirs – refer to a place. When this happens, we can call them *communities of place*: communities motivated by some form of interest and care for the space in which they find themselves, and that, with their presence and activity, and with the meanings they attribute to them, transform them into a place.

Box 1.2   Project-based communities

Contemporary communities are open, light, and intentional, born when traditional communities dissolve or encounter difficulties.[5] Let us take a closer look. Traditional communities (that we can call non-modern) are relatively closed social forms, connected to a place and characterized by networks of dense, stable, and lasting links. These communities, where they still exist, are important and we have much to learn from them. However, in contemporary societies (more precisely, in the parts of them affected by processes of modernization), these traditional communities no longer exist or are in serious crisis, leaving room for growing individualization (with all of the relevant implications in terms of solitude and individual and social fragility). In opposition to all of this, in recent years social innovation has produced a variety of new social forms, including the contemporary communities we refer to here.

Unlike non-modern communities, that were not chosen by their members, contemporary communities exist by choice. That is, they are intentional communities. At the same time, unlike the intentional communities of the 20th century, that were based on strong ideologies that required exclusive affiliation and promised a strong identity, contemporary intentional communities are multiple, non-exclusive and do not require a particular level of commitment. We must also note that they are not the communities often invoked by those who propose a return to the past (a past for which some may be nostalgic, but which in any case, cannot return), with a rhetoric that entails the proposal of closed communities, formed around identitarian positions that produce an "us" against others, and thus appear regressive and socially dangerous.

The contemporary communities to which we refer form around a theme that acts as a catalyst[6] and an idea to be realized through collaboration. Thus, they can also be defined as project-based communities and refer to the various specific themes to which this project applies (for example, there can be communities that work on food and food networks; on sports or recreational activities; on care for the person and the environment, and so on).[7] It follows that the construction of these communities de facto coincides with the definition and development of this project.

The ability of proximity to produce communities has an evident link with relational properties, but it also has a link with functional properties. Or more precisely, with the interaction that can take place based on an elementary principle of social psychology, defined as the "principle of proximity,"[8] according to which people tend to form social relationships with those who are closest to them. This is for the obvious reason that it is easier and more likely to start a conversation with someone next to you than someone far away.

It follows that a system of proximity in which a variety of functions can take place offers people more opportunities for encounters, more reasons to initiate a conversation, more motivations to start a project, and potentially, to construct a community.

1.3   Diversified proximity and specialized proximity

For each of us, proximity refers to the point in time and space in which we find ourselves. The point from which we look at the world and act on it. It follows that our capacity for action, our everyday life, our ability to think and realize our life projects always start from proximity; from the place where our body is physically located. In other words, we can live typing on a cell phone or computer, we can work and study and entertain ourselves online, and we can order everything we need the same way. But our body will always be part of a physical context that allows it to live and do everything that, by its nature, is unfailingly physical. This is why it is important to know what we can do in proximity; and how we can do it.

To discuss this, we can refer to a range of possibilities that are between two extremes. The first is *diversified proximity*, that offers many different opportunities and that allows for finding (almost) everything a person needs to live. At the other extreme we find *specialized proximity*, that beyond the essential functions of biological survival, offers only one possibility: a single service or a single type of activity (for example, to reside, work, study, spend free time, etc.). It follows that, to live in a world of specialized proximities, people must move from one place to another, from one specialized proximity to another.

In the history of humanity, there has been a continuous evolution of systems of proximity. More precisely, from the beginning until two centuries ago, they have gradually been integrated with new artifacts that have made possible – and at times pleasant – the life of human beings in environments far from those in which we emerged as a species at the beginning of our history.

Yet before efficient means of transport were available to everyone (and obviously, before connectivity) what we did every day had to be easy to reach by foot (or, for the few who could afford it, on means pulled by animals). That is, it had to be in proximity. For this reason, villages and neighborhoods in the pre-modern city necessarily had to offer a variety of functional and relational opportunities. That is, to use the terminology introduced before, they had to be characterized by a diversified proximity. We could call this condition pre-modern diversified proximity.

In the last two centuries, almost until current times, the situation has changed. Innovation in transportation and the first phase of telecommunications led to the territorial modification of the distribution of activities and services: in the name of management efficiency, the activities of coordination and direction were moved to central nodes and production and service activities to specialized nodes, and in the name of economies of scale, the latter grew continuously and thus referred to pools of labor (for production) and users (for the services) that in turn were increasingly large and referred to increasingly vast areas. All of this was done to seek efficiency in the single nodes, trusting that the people involved had the means of transport necessary to move from one of them to another, and without evaluating the sacrifices that would be requested of them in terms of time and health, or the diseconomies that it entailed for the sociotechnical system overall, or the environmental problems that ensued.

In actual fact, looking at things from the standpoint of the people involved, we see that in the search for the efficiency of the economic system (and in the name of what was presented as progress) they were pushed to continuously move from one place to another to find the specialized proximities in which it was possible to respond to their needs or desires (the proximity in which to work, that in which to return to sleep, that in which to spend Saturday evening, that in which there are administrative services, and so on). All of this led to the reduction of the possibility of encounters and aggregation around shared themes, with the consequent push towards increasingly individualistic behavior. In short, the spread of specialized proximity moved in parallel with the loss of significance of the relational dimension of proximity.

What has been described to this point is what, in reference to the theme of proximity, produced and left us the heritage of the last century. With the new century, the entire picture has begun to change, driven by three powerful agents of transformation: *technological innovation*, that has made it possible to imagine and create sociotechnical systems based on new ideas of proximity; *social innovation*, that has shown how these technical innovations make new social forms possible; and *cultural innovation*, that by rediscussing some principles of modernity, has laid the basis for a redefinition of the very idea of proximity. Lastly, the pandemic came, that made the fragility of our societies tangible for everyone, and by acting as a great social experiment, accelerated all of the processes underway.

1.4   Technical innovation and hybrid proximity

Technological innovation has recently opened up various possibilities. The substance of this change is well known: connectivity and digital technologies allow us to interact with people and objects anywhere in the world without moving from where we are. The results is that (almost) anything can be done (almost) anywhere. This unprecedented possibility can be oriented in two different directions: pushing the specialized proximities generated by the last century to the extreme, or producing new forms of diversified proximity: a *hybrid*, physical and digital proximity.

With respect to this second possibility, at this time, what is happening is the emergence of a scenario that we could define as *everything at/from home*, a scenario made practicable by the technical possibility to do (almost) everything at home and receive (almost) everything that we need at home. What this scenario offers us can appear to be very convenient for those who use its services, but it is very burdensome for those who are the providers of these services. That is, those who make the opaque machine work thanks to which what we think we need actually comes to our doorstep or our computer screen; to our proximity, that is.

Ultimately, this scenario of everything at/from home offers us a perspective that appears dystopian: by using technology to bring everything home (work, study, entertainment, products, and services), it pushes to the extreme the trend already underway for some time towards the individualization of people and their closure in the private realm. In practice, the rules of the game change, but the results remain and are amplified, that consist of the growth of consumption, environmental burden, inequality, solitude, and marginalization.[9]

However, this trajectory of innovation is not the only one. Another one emerged some time ago, that proposes an entirely different scenario: that of *everything in proximity*.

The first distinguishing aspect of this trajectory is the role of a new relational hybrid proximity. Digital technologies and connectivity, if ap propriately oriented, can have a role opposite of that described before, allowing for organizing encounters in proximity that otherwise would be unlikely to occur. This way, people who live in proximity, for whom it is not easy to meet, can use a digital platform to do something together: from organizing a soccer tournament or a neighborhood party, to coordinating their actions to assist a sick person. All of this helps construct communities, communities that refer to a place, a place where encounters occur in the physical world, but that could not exist if they were not supported by what happens in the digital world.

The second aspect that characterizes this scenario is that of making it possible and interesting to reorganize productive systems and services in a distributed form. Digital technologies and connectivity offer the possibility to bring a series of services and activities into proximity, i.e. near to interested people. By doing this, not only do they break the model of functional distancing and specialized proximity of the previous century, but they also distinguish themselves from the scenario of everything at/from home described before. What emerges is another possibility, that of everything close, everything in proximity; a hybrid proximity that, in this case, can become not only functional, but also relational. And this proximity combines the efficacy of having what is needed at a short distance, with the reduction of the environmental burden that follows. This also offers the possibility to reorganize the sociotechnical system in a distributed form, that is very important for the purposes of our discussion, and has numerous advantages on an individual level, but also in social, political, and environmental terms.

Box 1.3   Distributed systems

The expression *distributed system* can have various meanings. Here we refer to a sociotechnical system in which production and service activities are organized in small-scale units connected and distributed throughout an area. As a whole, they generate broader networks, yet without losing the relationship with the specific features of the places in which each node is located and of the communities that operate there.[10]

There is more than one reason to support the spread of this type of system.

Due to their nature as horizontal and decentralized systems, distributed systems allow for facing complexity by distributing it to their different nodes. This makes the systems more sensitive (to local specificities) and more flexible (in the presence of unforeseen developments) than vertical and centralized systems. For the same reason, they are able to adapt to the specific features of the contexts in which they are located and to be resilient with respect to possible crises. Furthermore, they also create the preconditions for a more fair and democratic society. By their nature, distributed systems make possible a fair distribution of value produced, promote local skills, and give motivation and meaning to local decision-making systems that, referring to distributed activities, have a greater possibility to recognize problems and opportunities, to discuss them and make decisions.

At the same time, despite proposing modes of doing and thinking that represent a radical break with the dominant modes (that dominated for all of the last century), the spread of distributed systems is a practicable scenario because it is based on a full utilization of the potential of contemporary technologies. More precisely, it can be seen as the result of three successive waves of technological innovation.

The first took place when the architecture of information systems went from the old hierarchical systems to network structures. This change began with the spread of distributed intelligence and with radical changes in the organizational systems that this made possible. The result is that the rigid and vertical organizational models that were dominant in industrialized society are blending into fluid and horizontal models, as new distributed forms of knowledge and decision-making processes gradually become more common.

The second wave of innovation has modified and is modifying energy systems. These changes are driven by the development of renewable energy sources, that by their nature are distributed, and for the development of small, high-efficiency power plants, renewable energy plants, and smart networks that connect them, creating models of distributed energy. The generation of distributed energy is one of the main components of a green economy that can be truly green. Thus it is reasonable to think that energy systems will follow the trajectory of information systems, increasingly shifting towards distributed system architectures.

The third wave of innovation towards distributed systems is opposed to vertical and globalized production and consumption systems. This field of innovation extends from the rediscovery of artisanal traditions and local agriculture to the hypothesis of network production systems based on new forms of production, such as those proposed by the movement of makers and fab labs. This form of distributed production has already had considerable success as regards food and agriculture, leading to the development of new relationships between urban and rural areas (from farmers' markets to community-supported agriculture, to the cases of urban farms, to everything that has been done under the slogan of "zero-mile food."). As regards manufacturing production, makers and fab labs have highlighted a field of opportunity that is still largely to be investigated, that calls into question the entire production system. The three waves of innovation have a common characteristic: they refer to a form of globalization aimed at using local resources and reducing the distances between production and utilization, between producers and users. This also creates the conditions for a new proximity.[11]

1.5 Social innovation and relational proximity

Living collaboratively, creating a community vegetable garden or green area, organizing support networks for the elderly and fragile, opening shared spaces for online work and workshops for traditional and digital artisanship, and seeking to revive a street or a neighborhood are all examples of social innovation that, explicitly or implicitly, refer to a place and enrich the system of proximity, in both its functional and relational dimensions.

Box 1.4 Social innovation

Social innovation exists when someone, changing a socially-consolidated way of doing things, resolves a problem or opens up new possibilities. A more precise definition could be: "We define social innovations as new ideas (products, services and models) that simultaneously meet social needs and create new social relationships or collaborations. In other words, they are innovations that are both good for society and enhance society's capacity to act."[12] The fact that this takes place, and the way in which it takes place, depend on the imagination, forward-thinking ability, and organizational skills of the promoters, as well as on the specific aspects of the moment and the context. Since the latter can be more or less favorable, social innovation does not appear linearly, but like all forms of innovation, proceeds by waves. And each of these waves of innovation has distinguishing aspects.

About fifteen years ago, the first signs were observed of what would become a great wave: groups of people who carried out new ideas on how to collaboratively face the problems that regarded them, and by doing so, contributed at the same time to regenerating the social fabric and sense of the places.[13] Examples could be found in all areas of daily life: from forms of living to those of working, from welfare to food networks, from cultural activities to the renewal of neighborhoods.

At the beginning, these initiatives were presented as constellations of creative communities: small groups of particularly active and dedicated people who were able to generate and implement a new idea on how to make something happen. With time, some groups and some ideas evolved: they spread, were consolidated, and encountered politicians and institutions that were able to recognize their value and support them. This produced other interesting political and institutional innovations that touched various themes and different scales.

After fifteen years of experience, today social innovation is no longer only carried out by small innovative groups (although they remain its core), but also takes place on the scale of large service systems (health, education, food, etc.) and that of entire cities (for examples, programs regarding the "15-minute city," to which this book refers). These activities are to be considered second level social innovations. They are possible because they emerge where there has been a long history of local, grassroots initiatives. And they have prospects for success if they are sustained by activities that, in turn, are local and come from the grassroots.

To present the reasoning for what has been stated, it is necessary to more carefully observe the way these social innovations function, considering the quality of the interactions on which they are based and the motivations that drive them. In doing so, a common trait emerges: all of the participants aspire to results that have practical value for them. But great importance is also given to other questions such as: the quality of the relationships they have, of the time used, of the work people are called on to do, and last, but not least, the quality of the place in which they occur. If this happens, it is because, in contrast with the dominating trends, those who participate produce relationships based on a renewed idea of care: care for people, places, and the environment. Care for what they do, and how they do it. On the other hand, experience tells us that there cannot be care without physical closeness; and thus without proximity.

This is exactly what social innovation shows us. Let us consider, for example, initiatives aimed at generating new modes of welfare: relational and collaborative welfare, in which all of the actors involved are and feel part of a community of care. We will return to this theme later (in Chapter 3). What interests us here is to note that these communities of care live in an ecosystem of places and spaces that, to perform the required role, must be physically proximate. Thus the proximity that is both functional and relational on which these communities are based also requires physical proximity. A similar argument can be applied to social innovation in work: reviving local business, new forms of digital or traditional artisanship, and neighborhood co-working for new online jobs can have success only if they are situated in the framework of a new economy of proximity, that sees them as nodes of a network of local relationships, thus able to produce communities of work with deep roots in their respective areas; and thus in conditions of proximity. Similar considerations could be developed in other areas of social innovation, for communities constructed around various common projects (for example, food networks, studying, or animating a street or a neighborhood). In each of these cases, declined differently depending on the theme, a close relationship could be found between the construction of community, care for what is being done, and proximity.

Overall, these social innovations can thus be seen as experiments on new ways of being and doing, that as regards the theme that interests us, not only aim to reconsider the value of proximity, but demonstrate in practice how that can be done.

All of this can be said observing the social innovations that have emerged in the last fifteen years, and that today, collectively, can be interpreted as a large wave of social innovation that has characterized the beginning of this century. In the meantime, however, the world has changed a great deal: environmental and social problems, that were recognized by few fifteen years ago, have become evident and tangible for everyone. And then the pandemic crisis came, that has made the overall view even more different than what it had been. In this new context, new forms of social innovation emerge that are characterized by stronger attention to environmental questions and the places in which they are situated. New communities of place are created that are active on themes that, more than in the past, integrate the social dimension and the environmental dimension.

1.6   Cultural innovation and more-than-human proximity

Social innovation intersects with a similarly important cultural innovation that, as regards its component that interests us most here, implies the ability to overcome the dualistic model that separates "nature" from "society," and recognizes the radical interdependence between everything that surrounds us. This implies, among other things, overcoming the anthropocentrism of the Western tradition and learning to see ourselves as part of the "web of life,"[14] i.e. as part of the mesh of interdependency that connects everything that contributes to life on earth[15]: a network of elements that exist not to support humans, but to allow for life on the planet. We are part of that life, but are not the center of it. In this spirit, the proximity we are speaking of tends to include everything that exists around us: not only other human beings and the products of human activity, but also everything that is living and non-living; and to do so taking into account that the system of proximity to which it refers is a broader subsystem that extends well beyond what is close to us, which is, in fact, the web of life.

Box 1.5   Systems of proximity and the web of life

How can we define a system of proximity when we want to consider it part of the web of life? If everything is connected with everything, is it possible and legitimate to do so?

To answer these questions, we will start from Edgard Morin, when he writes that, although it is true that everything is linked to everything, it is also true that not all links are equal.[16] So within a broader system, different subsystems can be identified with their own internal coherence. The ability to recognize them requires special skills and sensitivity.[17] At the same time, continues Morin, the way in which these systems can be identified, and thus the type of internal coherence recognized in them, also depends on the observer; on what the observer wants to know of them and what they intend to do with them. This means that, to identify and describe a system, a special ability is necessary that allows us to extract from the microsystem the subsystem that has its internal consistency and is coherent with our intentions.

Therefore, if the definition of the subsystems on which to operate is influenced by the way we look at them and consider them given our aim, we can say that these subsystems do not exist prior to our projects, but are the first step of them; the result of the project-oriented actions with which, based on our intentions and possibilities, we define what elements to consider as part of our range of action or not. To summarize: there is an element of intentionality in the way we imagine the subsystems on which to operate.

Therefore, in our case, the intentionality is that of recognizing as useful the activity of extracting from the planetary web of interdependencies the subsystem that includes everything that takes place close to us and of which we are a part; and to do so because we have reason to believe that, if we want to act on the world, we need to start with what is around us.

The discussion on how to understand and promote a more-than-human proximity has been underway for some time, but it has become broader and deeper as a result of the environmental catastrophes – and most recently the pandemic – that have led, and still are leading, to focusing attention on the fact that what until now we have called nature, can become an agent of extraordinary power in human affairs, at all levels, from the global level to each of our daily lives. These actions, that with Bruno Latour we can call "politics of nature," push us to change our ways of being and thinking; and they should push us to recognize that we are a part of life on earth. They should help us recognize that we are all *terrestrial*.[18]

Approaching this result (recognizing ourselves as terrestrial and behaving as a consequence) can take place through goals that are partial and incomplete, but able to make us take steps in the right direction. Those partial and incomplete steps, but oriented in the right direction, can be taken starting from the use of technologies able to make the economy circular and lessen its impact on the planet. But they can also take other paths. One example is that of a democracy that also gives a voice to non-human entities (animals, woods, rivers),[19] or to favor a new wave of social innovations motivated by the desire to regenerate the web of life.[20]

This last line of reflection leads us to introduce the concept of care into the discussion of proximity; not only its practical meaning of taking care of someone or something, but its philosophical meaning: care as a profound essence of the interdependence that keeps the web of life together.[21] And thus the system of proximity as one in which these interdependencies can, or cannot, take place (we will return to all of this in Chapter 3).

In this conceptual framework, the discussion on the meaning to give to the condition of diversified and relational proximity becomes fundamental for the construction of a culture of sustainability adequate for the dimension of the multiple crises in which we find ourselves. This can be a culture with the depth necessary to call into question some of the strongest anthropocentric, and thus intrinsically unsustainable, assumptions of modern Western culture.

1.7   Livable proximity

The three lines of innovation that we have recalled, merging together, indicate a direction to follow: a proximity that is diversified (because it includes multiple functions), relational (because it is based on the interaction between functional and relational properties), and hybrid (not only because the physical component is supported by the digital component, but also because what is traditionally considered "culture" is recognized as part of what is traditionally called "nature").

This notion of proximity offers many possibilities (in terms of services, work, and social and cultural activities), characterized by a dynamic interaction of functional and relational properties and integrated by a digital infrastructure that supports local activities and connects it to global networks.

This is a proximity in which interactions of care take place between people and between everything living and non-living that makes up the web of life. Therefore, it is a *livable proximity* in the deepest and fullest sense of the word, because it is able to offer us much, if not all, of what we need to live sustainably: from biological life to the way of answering the questions and desires of daily life, to the search for the meaning of our existence.

How can we go in this direction? It depends on the context, obviously. In this book the choice is to consider the urban context, and by using the filter of proximity in its different dimensions, to construct scenarios. Among these, the most desirable is the scenario of the *city of proximity*.

Notes

[1] R. Boschma, "Proximité et innovation," Économie Rurale, 280(1), 2004, pp. 8-24; R. Boschma, P.-A. Balland, M. de Vaan, "The Formation of Economic Networks: A Proximity Approach," in A. Torre, F. Wallet (eds.), *Regional Development and Proximity Relations*, Cheltenham, Edward Elgar, 2014, pp. 243-267; A.M. Lis, "Development of Proximity in Cluster Organizations," *Entrepreneurship and Sustainability Issues*, 8(2), 2020, pp. 116-132.

[2] Fritjof Capra, *The Web of Life. A New Scientific Understanding of Living Systems*, New York, Anchor Books, 1996 (Italian trans. *La rete della vita*, Milan, BUR, 2006); Donna Haraway, *Staying with the Trouble. Making Kin in the Chulucene*, Durham, Duke University Press, 2016 (Italian trans. *Chthulucene. Sopravvivere su un pianeta infetto*, Rome, Nero, 2019).

[3] G. Marocchi, "Cosa è la prossimità," www.confinionline.it, March 6, 2017; and Idem, "Comunità di prossimità, la condivisione riduce le distanze," www.labsus.org, September 5, 2016.

[4] Ezio Manzini, *Politiche del quotidiano*, Milan, Edizioni di Comunità, 2018.

[5] Ibid.

[6] Using the terminology introduced by Bruno Latour, they are groups of persons gathered around a *matter of concern*. Bruno Latour, *We Have Never Been Modern*, Cambridge, Harvard University Press, 1993 (orig. ed. *Nous n'avons jamais été modernes. Essai d'anthropologie symétrique*, Paris, Éd. La Découverte, 1991; Italian trans. *Non siamo mai stati moderni. Saggio di antropologia simmetrica*, Milan, Elèuthera, 1995).

[7] Manzini, *Politiche del quotidiano*, cit.

[8] T.M. Newcomb, "Varieties of Interpersonal Attraction," in D. Cartwright, A. Zander (eds.), *Group Dynamics: Research and Theory*, Row, Peterson & Co., 1960.

[9] Moreover, in the name of efficiency, the organizations that manage the systems become larger and larger (and thanks to the "winner take all" effect, the networks become enormously larger).

[10] Ezio Manzini, Mugendi M'Rithaa, "Distributed Systems and Cosmopolitan Localism. An Emerging Design Scenario for Resilient Societies," *Sustainable Development*, 24(5) (Special Issue: *The Cultural Dimension of Sustainability and Resilience*), September/October 2016, pp. 275-280.

[11] Ezio Manzini, "SLOC: The Emerging Scenario of Small, Open, Local, Connected," in S. Harding (ed.), *Grow Small, Think Beautiful. Ideas for a Sustainable World from Schumacher College*, Edinburgh, Floris Books, 2011, pp. 216-231; Manzini, M'Rithaa, "Distributed systems and cosmopolitan localism," cit.

[12] Robin Murray, Julie Caulier Grice, Geoff Mulgan, *Open Book of Social Innovation*, London, Nesta & the Young Foundation, 2010.

[13] Anna Meroni, *Comunità Creative, Creative Communities: People Inventing Sustainable Ways of Living*, Milan, Edizioni PoliDesign, 2007; Ezio Manzini, *Design, When Everybody Designs*, Cambridge (MA), The MIT Press, 2015.

[14] Capra, *The Web of Life*, cit.

[15] Arturo Escobar, *Designs for the Pluriverse. Radical Interdependence, Autonomy, and the Making of Worlds*, Durham, Duke Press, 2018; Haraway, *Staying with the Trouble*, cit.

[16] Edgar Morin, *The Method. Volume 1: the Nature of Nature*, New York, Peter Lang, 1992 (orig. ed. *La méthode. Tome 1. La Nature de la Nature*, Paris, Éditions du Seuil, 1977; Italian trans. *Il metodo. 1: La natura della natura*, Milan, Raffaello Cortina, 2001).

[17] E. Morin in Sacha Kagan, *Art and Sustainability: Connecting Patterns for a Culture of Complexity*, Bielefeld-London, Transcript Verlag, 2011, p. 132.

[18] Bruno Latour, *The Politics of Nature. How to Bring the Sciences into Democracy*, Cambridge, Harvard University Press, 2004 (orig. ed. *Politiques de la nature. Comment faire entrer les sciences en démocratie*, Paris, Éd. La Découverte, 1999; Italian trans. *Politiche della natura. Per una democrazia delle scienze*, Milan, Raffaello Cortina, 2000); Idem, *Down to Earth. Politics in the New Climate Regime*, Cambridge, Polity Press, 2018 (orig. ed. *Où atterrir? Comment s'orienter en politique*, Paris, Éd. La Découverte, 2017; Italian trans. *Tracciare la rotta. Come orientarsi in politica*, Milan, Raffaello Cortina, 2018).

[19] This can be done by researchers and scientists, but also by amateur groups, in the context of "citizen science" initiatives, and by activists of environmental movements. The expression "citizen science" indicates activities linked to sci-

entific research in which a network of citizens participate as amateurs. See G. Agnello, A. Sforzi, A. Berditchevskaia, *Verso una strategia condivisa per la citizen science in Italia. Doing It Together Science*, 2018, pdf available at https://discovery.ucl.ac.uk/.

[20] Ezio Manzini, Virginia Tassinari, "Designing Down to Earth. Lessons Learnt from Transformative Social Innovation," *Journal of Design and Culture*, in the course of publication.

[21] Maria Puig de la Bellacasa, *Matters of Care. Speculative Ethics in More Than Human Worlds*, Minneapolis-London, University of Minnesota Press, 2017.

2 The City of Proximity

In the great series of frescoes *Allegory and Effects of Good and Bad Government*, that Ambrogio Lorenzetti painted in Siena in 1338, on the wall depicting Good Government, we see what was thought to be a well-governed city at that time: a city that was compact, full of public and private places in which various groups of people were engaged in a variety of productive and reproductive activities; a complex city that bubbled with life, surrounded by a countryside in turn rich and diversified.

The well-governed city that Lorenzetti shows us thus has characteristics that in many ways make it similar to what we could define today as a city of proximity: a city on a human scale, that is dense and diversified in its functions, characterized by public spaces and a mix of residential and productive activities; a city in which the value of proximity is evident in both its functional and relational dimensions; a city that is livable because, as in Lorenzetti's depiction, the proximity found there is amply diversified, since everything you can want, and want to do, is close by.

After recognizing this similarity between what the fresco shows us and what we could indicate as the city of proximity and its good government, we can also observe the differences.

2.1   The city of common goods

Between the good government of almost seven hundred years ago and what we would like to propose today, there are in fact similarities, but also profound differences.

The first difference has to do with the nature and modalities of evolution of the set of norms, conventions, and shared visions that constitute the terrain on which all of the civic activities that represent good government can take place; and that, as a whole, contribute to forming the social common goods on which and with which a city is made.

In Lorenzetti's times, and until the last century, these common goods were constructed slowly, over time; so slowly as to appear to the people involved as an almost natural occurrence, whose existence did not require an explicit, conscious project. And good government could therefore be considered as administration and care for a given heritage. Today, in a connected world in rapid and deep transformation, the traditional way of regenerating and managing common goods in general, and of the common good of the city in particular, does not function anymore. Therefore, what in the past appeared as a quasi-natural process must become the result of conscious actions of design. We can call the results *intentional common goods*: common goods produced by choice, that emerge from an activity that, by all means, can be considered a project.

The second fundamental difference between the city of proximity we speak of today and that depicted by Lorenzetti is strictly linked to what we have just said about common goods: in the 14th century, the urban density and diversified proximity that we see in the fresco were a forced choice. In fact, in a world without mass transit and without connectivity, a city could not be otherwise; people needed to be close, and to have everything they needed close by. Today, on the other hand, the contemporary version of this diversified proximity is an option. It is one of the possible choices. Thus, in parallel with what we have said for common goods, contemporary proximity, when we want it, must also be the result of specific project-based choices. In other words, it is *intentional proximity*.

Finally, there is another observation to be made, that makes the difference between then and now even deeper: the proximity of Lorenzetti's city was a quality of the physical world. More precisely, he referred to a system of proximity that operated in a well-defined physical space. To the contrary, in the contemporary city the system of proximity we speak of is also located in a digital space. Thus the proximity we must consider, as we saw in Chapter 1, is a proximity that is not only intentional but also hybrid.

Having highlighted the deep differences between common goods and proximity in the 1300s and today, it should be noted that, today as then, the theme of proximity remains linked to that of common goods, and we can say that the city of proximity is also the city of common goods: there is no common good without a community that cares for it. And there is

Box 2.1   Common goods and community

In the most widespread definition, common goods are those that are shared by the members of a community. In general, we refer to a variety of goods that are fundamental for our existence, starting with natural physical goods (such as water and air), to arrive at intangible social goods (such as mutual trust, widespread competences, and the perception of security that characterizes a city), passing through various types of tangible social common goods (such as streets, squares, and public gardens when there is a community that assumes the responsibility to care for them).

The conceptualization of common goods has a long history. Regarding sustainability, the expression is used often, and has been for years by numerous authors. Yet only recently has the concept been recognized by many as a main theme of every possible strategy for the future. This renewed interest began with Elinor Ostrom, with her studies and the Nobel Prize in Economics given to her in 2009.[1] Then, many other authors, such as Stefano Rodotà, Silke Helfrich, Michel Bauwens, David Bollier, Giorgio Arena, Christian Iaione, and Sheila Foster brought it into the political debate and the discussion of social innovation.[2] And the encounter between common goods and urban regeneration – that was decisive – took place in Bologna, in 2015, in the context of the first thematic conference on urban common goods of the International Association for the Study of the Commons (IASC).

A more precise definition, that is useful for the theme we are developing here, is offered to us by Carlo Donolo: common goods are "a set of necessarily shared goods. They are goods because they allow for the development of social life, the resolution of collective problems, and the existence of human beings in their relationships within the ecosystems of which they are a part. They are shared because … they are better and express their best qualities when they are treated and governed as "common" goods, accessible to everyone, at least in principle."[3]

This definition highlights the fact that to have a common good there must be a community. There is in fact a dual relationship between the two: the common good allows for "the development of social life," that is, it feeds and regenerates the community. At the same time, though, the community governs it "in common" and thus implicitly and explicitly defines the rules for doing so. This leads to another important aspect: not all public goods are common goods, and not all common goods are public. An abandoned and mistreated square is a public good, but it is not a common good, because there is no community that takes care of it. A neighborhood garden, managed by the residents themselves, is a common good even when the land it occupies is private.

no community capable of care that is not a part of a system of proximity, understood as the sum of common goods that allow it to exist.

This same double link between common good and community is found analogously for *social common goods*: mutual trust, collaborative capabilities, widespread competences, and perception of security, for example, exist – as do all common goods – thanks to a community that creates them and regenerates them. And at the same time they constitute the weft and warp of every possible social fabric and thus every community; without them, society would literally not hold together. On the other hand, since like all common goods, they also cannot be established by decree, their existence and their quality emerge from a complex sum of activities, conversations, and regenerative projects that, in turn, must take place in a system of proximity that enables them. Thus, there are double links that connect not only common goods and communities, but also both to the system of proximity. As we were saying, the city of common goods is also the city of proximity.

Considering the city of proximity as a common good means recognizing it as a social and material resource (a human-non-human aggregate) that belongs to all of its citizens; and that all of its citizens contribute to producing, and must care for. This means recognizing that there is not only the city of the market (of goods and consumption), nor only that of the state (of its local institutions, its rules, and the public spaces they generate). The market and the state produce the city, but cannot define it entirely. There is also, in fact, the city of physical and social common goods, that in order to exist requires appropriate conditions of proximity.

In practice, adopting this point of view means assuming that the city is not a sum of services to access (because people have the means or the right to do so). Rather, it is a complex organism of which the citizens themselves are an active and collaborative part.

The problem that is posed is thus the following: how to regenerate a city of common goods in contemporary hybrid proximity?

To respond, we will start from another image of the city, an image that is far from that of good government, and also from the city of proximity and of common goods towards which we would like to move: that of the city of modernity of the last century, that we could call the city of distances and of the crisis of common goods.

2.2   The city of distances and its crisis

The cities of last century were constructed around the idea of efficiency based on specialization and economies of scale: in the name of efficiency, some areas of the city were specialized (for work, leisure, studying, and returning home to sleep). Here, in these areas, is where, in the name of economies of scale, the supply of, and thus the demand for, a specific type of activities and services were concentrated.

Indeed, at the time this idea of specialization of areas of the city was introduced, production activities, that operate on a large-scale and generate pollution, were to be segregated far from residential areas. But office work was also to be aggregated to facilitate the flow of information, that at the time could take place (almost) only through physical presence. Then the idea took hold that in order to be efficient, and thus to offer more at lower prices, commerce also had to take place in large shopping centers. Finally, the same approach was extended to all areas of daily life, from hospitals to schools, from sports complexes to recreation areas. The result of this territorial specialization of activities and services was that people and goods had to continuously move between one specialized area and another; that is, between one functional proximity and another. What emerged was a city of continuous mobility of objects and persons: the *city of distances.*

For many decades, the dominant thinking was that all of this worked very well; that this mobility and the consequent traffic, pollution, harm to health, and territorial uprooting of citizens were sacrifices to be accepted in the name of general progress, the well-being of everyone, and the economic health of the system. In that spirit, even the economic cost of these problems was considered an inevitable diseconomy to be externalized among the entire society.

Seen with today's eyes, that is, with the experience gained in the meantime, with the environmental and social sensitivity that has since evolved, and with the new opportunities that technology has made available, the entire apparatus on which the city of distances was constructed no longer holds up; not only do we now recognize that the diseconomies we mentioned have reached unsustainable levels, but the reasons that led to proposing that type of specialization, and that type of large aggregation of activities and services, have also been greatly reduced, if not even reversed in some cases. Lastly, as we have seen (section 1.4), the technological conditions have been created that make it thinkable and possible to dismantle large monofunctional centers, distribute activities and services throughout the territory, and rearrange different functions at the local level creating new forms of diversified proximity.

Recently, the pandemic and its effects have accelerated the crisis of the city of distances. The health distancing required of us has shown everyone how important the local distribution of services is, as well as the possibility to work from home or close to home; and how much we need to know the people next door.

2.3   Competing scenarios

Faced with environmental emergencies, social crises, the current possibilities of technology and the new demands posed by the pandemic, today different ideas of the city and different strategies of development co-exist and clash: there are those who tend to continue, and adapt, the city of modernity from the last century (the city of distances). And there are those who propose to direct its evolution towards new perspectives.

Adopting the criterion of proximity as a method of interpretation, and remembering what we said in Chapter 1 in regard to the evolutionary trajectories of proximity, we can outline two scenarios: that of the city of everything at/from home, and that of the city of proximity, which is our scenario of reference.

The principal characteristics of the *city of everything at/from home* are connected to what has been mentioned previously by discussing the new proximity made possible by digital technologies and connectivity (section 1.4). In functional terms, in this scenario the city continues to be considered a mega-machine to produce results, but now it is a machine that, having new technologies available, presents itself as a platform of (online and offline) services. Its strength is having on its side the economic interests which have already invested in it (and that have already accumulated enormous fortunes). That is not all, though: the direction it proposes appears to be in line with the search for individual well-being, easily accessible through a series of products and services. For those who play the role of consumers of those products and users of those services, what this scenario proposes can thus appear to be very convenient. Presented this way, though, the scenario of everything at/from home leaves in the background the state of objective servitude in which it places those who work to make those products and services available. And the same is true for the environmental and social effects of this ease of use for the end user.

Ultimately, for everything that surrounds the user, that is, for everything that is not in their private space, what this scenario proposes is a social desert: a non-city made up of an aggregate of individuals without communities, without common goods, and without place; a large machine for individual consumption that offers those who receive the services convenience in exchange for solitude and control. And it does so based on an economic and organizational model that is unsustainable in both environmental and social terms.

The second scenario, that of the city of proximity, proposes a city whose full extension is characterized by a diversified, relational, and hybrid proximity, in contrast with the city of specialized and functional proximity of the last century, and with that of the new proximity of everything at/from home, of which we just spoke.

In the subsequent sections, we will use the conceptualization of proximity proposed in the previous chapter to discuss the implications regarding the city and its generative processes. Before proceeding, it can be useful to stress that the background on which it is based has been co-generated by the social innovation of the last twenty years and scientific and philosophical research on how to rethink the role of human beings in the web of life (see what is presented in sections 1.5 and 1.6). This implies a radical change in the way of conceiving the functioning of the city: from the city seen as a mega-machine, to the city as a complex ecosystem. Consistent with this approach, the city of proximity should be understood as encompassing multiple *proximities* in the plural; the city we are speaking of emerges from a search for proximity in all of the ways it can present itself.

2.4   Everything in less than 15 minutes, but not only

Considering its functional dimension, the city of proximity appears to us, first of all, as a technical and social platform thanks to which everything we need and everything we have to do daily is a few minutes away by foot or bicycle from where we live.

This first description of the properties of the city of proximity has the merit of being simple and clear; and it allows for immediately recognizing some of its possible qualities. It is a city that, by eliminating obligatory mobility, reduces traffic (and the resulting pollution), and thus returns time of life and public spaces to people; the time that was previously used to go to work, to distant shopping malls and municipal offices, and the streets, squares, and sidewalks that were previously occupied by automobiles. Thus the city of proximity is also a city that allows children to go to school by foot and to play in the streets, and the elderly to feel safe when they walk around and to have everything they need in the vicinity.

This idea of city is certainly not new. Its roots are to be found in the idea of the "neighborhood unit" proposed at the start of the last century[4] and, since then, it has been taken into consideration for various cities in the world. Moreover, in many other cities, steps have been taken in this same direction. The idea saw a strong revival with "la Ville du quart d'heure" proposed in 2019 by Carlos Moreno, a French-Columbian professor who works in Paris, and by the mayor Anna Hidalgo, for whom Moreno is a consultant, who made it the core proposal of her (victorious) campaign for re-election as mayor of the French capital in 2020. This choice was made because the "15-minute city" formula was found to be an effective representation of the sum of what the city administration had done in the previous term (initiatives for pedestrianization, development of alternative mobility, new green areas and new infrastructure) and could provide an effective framework to move in that same direction in the subsequent term: extend the idea of the 15-minute city to the entire urban area, thus improving the quality of life for all citizens, and at the same time contributing to reaching the goals of the Paris Agreement on climate.

It should be said, although Paris is the city in which this program has been adopted most explicitly, that there are other cities that, with more or less conviction and not necessarily using this expression, have been moving in the same direction. C40 (an organization that coordinates climate initiatives in many large cities around the world[5]) names ten such cities, including Barcelona, Milan, Shanghai, Houston, and Ottawa, to which we can add Melbourne and Detroit.[6]

Example 1 *Paris and the 15-minute city*

In 2020, the 15-minute city was at the center of the re-election campaign of Paris mayor Anne Hidalgo. The main reasons for this choice were: to reduce atmospheric pollution (seeking to become a zero-emissions city by 2050) and to increase Parisians' quality of life (improving air quality and reducing the hours lost for obligatory movements in the city).

The program foresaw new bicycle paths, the elimination of most parking places on the streets, new office and coworking spaces in neighborhoods lacking them; the use of infrastructure and buildings outside of standards hours; support for neighborhood shops, the creation of small parks in school courtyards, and opening them to the local population outside of school hours. All of this has the aim of transforming the city into a constellation of neighborhoods in which everything needed for daily life is present.

In reality, those goals were mostly the continuation of programs already underway, but that were presented as a unitary vision on the occasion of the mayoral elections: the 15-minute city. Among these programs, the best-known and most visible is the construction of a large bicycle infrastructure, as the first phase of the *Plan Vélo*, the ambitious plan that for the coming years aims to provide the city with 1,000 km of bike paths. For the purposes of our discussion, though, it is interesting to mention two other programs.

The first is the transformation of the courtyards of many schools into small parks, and opening them to local residents outside of school hours. This is an initiative that has all of the characteristics of a social innovation project of proximity. It is in fact a light, diffused intervention that makes better use of an existing resource (school courtyards) over the course of the day. By doing this, it enriches the system of proximity with a new function (the micro-park of proximity) and gives schools a new role in neighborhood life (becoming multi-use spaces, open to different social groups).

The other program that is very interesting for us regards the traditional neighborhood commercial and artisanal activities, that not only receive help to remain alive, but also to review and revise their way of operating, adapting to the transformations that have taken place, and those currently underway. For this purpose, an agency has been created[7] with the specific task of supporting merchants and artisans that operate in the neighborhoods (for example, the agency can purchase spaces for shops or rent them at an accessible price to those who wish to open activities in proximity, also helping new entrepreneurs to develop their projects, if necessary).

The recent success of this idea and its acceleration have more than one motivation. The most evident, long-term reasons are, obviously, the growth of traffic and the pollution it generates, and the time wasted moving around, with the resulting stress. In addition to these environmental and health motivations that citizens can immediately perceive, others have been added over time. As stated, the maturity and spread of connectivity and digital technologies have made it technically possible to bring services closer to users and to bring work activities to neighborhoods and homes thanks to distributed systems (we discussed this in Box 1.3). This meant that what could have seemed a utopia before, began to appear as a prospect that was practicable, and for some, economically interesting. Lastly, the Covid-19 catastrophe acted as a great social experiment, in which many people were pushed to work online from home or close to home, to make use of neighborhood stores, and to take walks and spend their free time in their own neighborhoods. Thus, not only did the pandemic highlight the importance of local services (which for us means the importance of services of proximity), but it also showed that it was possible to change habits and rediscover the value of proximity.

To more precisely characterize this proposal, this is how the official site of the C40 association presents the principles on which it is based:[8]

1. the residents of each neighborhood have easy access to goods and services, in particular food products, including fresh food, and health care;
2. each neighborhood has various types of dwellings, of different sizes and levels of economic accessibility, so as to be able to house different types of families and allow many people to live closer to where they work;
3. the residents of each neighborhood can breathe clean air without harmful pollutants, and there are green areas to be enjoyed;
4. many residents have the possibility to work close to home or online, thanks to the presence in the neighborhood of offices, shops, and coworking spaces.

The integration of these principles leads to formulating a vision of the city and to identifying the steps to implement it. The vision is that of a polycentric city that realizes the promise of the 15-minute city throughout the entire territory. The first step to be taken to reach this goal consists of intervening on mobility and the distribution of services, and at the same time, operating in proximity, to reorient and coordinate various urban functions: pre-schools, schools, health care facilities, green areas, and public spaces.

An entire generation of services and service locations must be rethought and new urban common goods must emerge. In that regard, Carlos Moreno writes: "This is another way to live the city; a way in which the social link that is created in proximity can become part of a better quality of life. This means restoring the most precious characteristic of the city: that of being a living universe. And restoring its metabolism, as we would do for every living organism, to make the city alive and available to everyone."[9]

2.5   Functional proximity and "minimum ecological units"

To give a more concrete form to what has been presented to this point, we can consider another significant case: that of the *Superilles* of Barcelona (*superilla* means superblock in Catalan, i.e. a system composed of various blocks). The initial idea was proposed more than thirty years ago by Salvador Rueda (the founder and director of the Urban Ecology Agency of Barcelona) and was the subject of various experiments, with an acceleration in recent years, during the administration of mayor Ada Colau. This program led to the transformation of some neighborhoods (first Born and Gràcia, then Poblenou, and lastly Sant Antoni) in a process of gradual learning such that the last *superilla*, Sant Antoni, is a good example of what a neighborhood of a 15-minute city could be today (that in this case, is actually less than 10 minutes).

Having identified and defined the area on which to operate, the first intervention was to change the traffic flows, reducing and slowing down the passage of vehicles on internal streets. This first action should not be seen, though, as only an action on mobility, but also, and above all, as the recapture by the citizens of public spaces (those previously occupied principally by cars and parking places). Rueda says: "In this moment, for most planners, the most important thing is to create pedestrian areas. Not for me. I want to create citizens' areas."[10] And he explains: being pedestrians regards a means of transport, and the street is only used to move. For the citizen, however, the street can be much more: a public space to be used in various ways. In fact, Rueda's central idea was not to remove cars from the streets to give the streets to the pedestrians, but to eliminate the mono-functionality of the streets themselves. The streets within the Superilles are to be transformed into mixed-use, shared public spaces, in which different types of citizens can meet each other, different activities can take place, and different forms of mobility can co-exist. In other words, if the streets and squares become platforms of opportunity, this becomes a starting point to prepare a series of other possible activities: gardens, play areas for children, places for festivals and concerts, and meeting spaces.

In turn, this stimulates a broader range of convergent public policies: housing policies, to avoid processes of ghettofication and/or gentrification, and to the contrary, that are able to guarantee social diversity; food policies, that lead to redesigning networks of food production and consumption from the perspective of greater food self-sufficiency of the city; labor policies, oriented towards a new economy of proximity, that revitalizes shops and artisanal and traditional industrial activities, coordinating them with the new activities of digital artisanship and with opportunities introduced by the territorial redistribution of work online; and policies for the regeneration of the democratic life of the city, starting from its molecular neighborhood dimension, leading to that of the city as a whole and to the now unavoidable dimension of the collection, processing, and possession of data relating to the city and its citizens. In Barcelona, all of this has begun.

Example 2 *Barcelona and the Superilles*

The program aims to create a network of macro-blocks in the city of Barcelona, the Superilles. The resulting urban model consists of the merger of nine blocks (3X3), starting with the street grid designed by Ildefonso Cerdà in the mid 1800s with his plan for urban expansion. On the perimeter of these Superilles, there are roads for fast transport and public networks, while the internal streets allow only for slow circulation, favoring pedestrian and bicycle mobility. Automobiles can come in, but at a speed of less than 10 km an hour, they have only a single lane, and street parking has been eliminated. This frees most of the streets of cars, making them public spaces available for other activities.

Salvador Rueda's original idea dates back to thirty years ago, and the program was initiated by the administrations that preceded the current one led by mayor Ada Colau, with some initial experiments: the first in 1993 in the Born neighborhood, then two others in Gràcia in 2005. In 2015, the new Colau administration decided to go forward with the program, first reviving it with experimentation in the Poblenou neighborhood and then in 2018 in Sant Antoni. In November 2020, the administration announced that it had opened a new phase of the Superilles program. The goal is ambitious: extend the transformation of Sant Antoni to the entire area of the Eixample, practically all of the central and historical area of the city. "In the coming years," according to a City of Barcelona release, "the Superblock idea will be gradually extended with the participation of the citizens, creating a network of 21 green hubs and 21 neighborhood squares, and gaining 33.4 hectares of pedestrian space and an additional 6.6 hectares of green."[11]

The design and development of all of the interventions of the Superilles program, especially the most recent ones, involved the inhabitants in the co-design of new public spaces (obtained by freeing the streets from automobiles) and the new services that it was gradually decided to add. All of the social actors potentially interested participated in these activities: in addition to the public entity coordinating the project, the inhabitants (as single individuals and as spontaneous and organized groups), the commercial businesses operating in the area, and third sector organizations. This collaborative design activity was also supported by a digital platform, called Decidim,[12] that is the result of another significant project by the city.

On an operational level, the transformation of the physical spaces was conceived in two phases: initially, the interventions were implemented in a light, reversible form (so they were inexpensive, easy to carry out, and if necessary, easy to change or dismantle). This "tactical" approach was chosen consistent with the experimental and participatory character of the initiative. In this first phase, concrete situations were created, on a real (and thus livable) scale, in which everyone could get an idea of how things could be. And thus everyone could intervene with criticisms and proposals. Once the ideas on how people wanted things to be were consolidated, there was a shift from the tactical phase to the implementation of the interventions to be decided in their definitive form.

As a whole, the program can be seen as a process of social learning, that took place on two levels: that which contributed to defining the characteristics of each intervention starting from an intense social conversation between the people involved, and that which, over the course of decades, allowed for learning how to best determine the different, subsequent interventions, thus going from a model of a city, that was interesting but abstract, to its practical realization, in all of its complexity.

However, the 15-minute city, the city of the Superilles described to this point, does not exhaust the question of the city of proximity, seen in its functional dimension. What we have cited to this point are in fact steps in a direction that, in order to be truly pursued, requires a double change of perspective. The first implies reconsidering services of proximity – or at least many of them – as collaborative services able to produce communities, thus giving concrete form to the idea of the city of common goods (see Box 2.1). The second change in perspective is to consider the city as an urban ecosystem composed of multiple local ecosystems of proximity connected with each other: "minimum ecological units"[13] whose metabolism in terms of flows of water, energy, food, and other materials is the most efficient possible and tends towards self-sufficiency. Adopting this approach, the city becomes a complex and resilient system precisely because it is composed of various interconnected ecosystems.[14] Having carried out this double change in perspective, systems of proximity, and thus the cases we have taken as examples, can be seen as concrete steps towards a city understood as an ecosystem composed of minimum ecological units.

Adopting this approach, the 15-minute city becomes a strategy for the ecological transition of cities. And it is such because it combines the motivations of citizens in terms of quality of life, with the need – more urgent than ever today – to reorient the evolution of cities themselves in an environmental direction. More precisely, it provides at the same time: a shared vision for bottom-up social innovation; a direction to follow, from above, to redesign the city's physical and social infrastructure; and indications on how to catalyze and coordinate the necessary social, political, and economic resources. This requires governance able to stimulate and support the resources available to the city; and first of all, the active and collaborative participation of citizens and their different forms of aggregation. In order for this to take place, a new wave of innovations must emerge that, from the beginning, are the result of the convergence of social, technical, cultural, and institutional innovation.

2.6   Relational proximity, local networks, and cosmopolitism

Providing many different occasions for encounters, the city of proximity, intended as diversified and relational proximity, offers its citizens not only greater opportunities for encounters, but also more reasons to begin a conversation and more motivations to imagine a project; and thus to construct communities, understood here as project-based communities (see Box 1.2).

This stated intention to create the most favorable conditions for mending the social fabric and the construction of communities is what distinguishes the city of proximity from other scenarios with which it competes: both the city of distances, in which the specialization of systems of proximity translates into distance between people, and the new proximity of everything at/from home, in which the same result is obtained by pushing people to self-segregate in their own private spaces.

The city of proximity is thus where short networks are cultivated thanks to which citizens are less alone and have more possibilities to express their capabilities by collaborating with others. On the other hand, since empathy, care, capability, and motivation to collaborate cannot be directly designed, it is necessary to discuss how it is possible to create the conditions to make their existence more likely. Before doing so, though, we must concentrate for a moment on the overall view, touching on a crucial point.

Up to now, we have seen that in the scenario proposed, *short networks* of daily life are cultivated. But that is not all. In this scenario, short networks are interwoven with *long networks* that connect the system of proximity with the rest of the city and the world. This interweaving is what distinguishes the relational proximity of this scenario from what it was in the pre-modern village. And this is what makes it fertile ground for cultural production, artistic creativity, and design thinking.

Considering that description of the scenario, a question emerges: it is possible to achieve it? Is it possible to cultivate at the same time the short networks of daily life and the long networks of opening to the world? In regard to this question, there can be different attitudes.

Some dream of a return to the past and a pre-modern proximity. So for them, the problem does not exist: they would be very happy to have a proximity of only short networks. But whether we like it or not, this perspective is impracticable, because in any case, the past cannot return: the social, cultural, and technological changes are such that the villages and neighborhoods of past centuries can certainly no longer be produced. However, despite being unattainable, this is a dangerous dream: it can generate ideas and behavior that lead to the construction of closed, identitarian communities, that in turn, can feed and be fed by regressive ideas and political practices.

For others, the problem that the question raises is serious and worrying. For them, the cultivation of short networks of daily life is in opposition to the possibility to open up to the world, and thus proximity is a synonym of closure and provincialism. But there are reasons to believe that this position is unjustifiably pessimistic. Obviously, there is no mathematical formula to prove the contrary; and there is no recipe that guarantees, in each case, the possibility to create short and long networks. However, we can recall, as Domenico De Masi does,[15] that "the Florence of the Medicis was a small city with less than 20,000 inhabitants, yet in the course of just a few decades it created the Renaissance." In other words, such a small city, in which everyone knew each other and everything that was needed for daily life was certainly close to home, was able to generate one of the greatest cultural revolutions in history. In the same spirit, we could add that Andy Warhol and most of the New York artists of his time were in Greenwich Village, a place that at the time was in many ways truly a sort of urban village, despite being in the center of Manhattan.

Naturally, there are a thousand evident reasons why these examples could not be reproduced today. Yet they tell us that cities with short distances and neighborhood networks can also be a favorable environment for dynamism, opening, and creativity. Therefore: if all of this took place in the past, in some cases, why could it not happen in the future?

Perhaps the question posed above could be changed and reformulated as follows: which has a greater possibility to be lively and dynamic: a city of individuals overwhelmed with the need to continuously move through traffic, or who are closed and connected in their homes, or a city of individuals and communities who live and operate in the open and connected neighborhoods that we can imagine and experiment with today?

The city of proximity we are speaking of is based on the conviction that the second option is more likely; and thus that this scenario can represent a contemporary expression of the *cosmopolitan localism*[16] that has been discussed for many years, and that maybe now we can begin to realize.

Box 2.2   Cosmopolitan localism

Observing contemporary society, we can see that, contrary to what was thought in the past, the joint phenomena of globalization and connectivity have given new meaning to what is local. The adjective "local" now refers to something very different from what was meant in the past: the valley, the agricultural village, the small provincial town, all isolated and relatively closed in their own cultures and economies. In fact, the term local now combines the specific characteristics of the places and their communities with new phenomena generated and sustained around the world by globalization and cultural and socioeconomic interconnection. Today these phenomena are often characterized by extremely negative trends, that go from regressive positions, that support a short-sighted vision of local interests, hidden behind the protective veil of traditions and identity,[17] to those that in the name of local development tend to transform what remains of local traditions, landscapes, and cultures into tourist attractions, generating what can be called a "Disneyfication" of local areas.[18]

Fortunately, there is not only this. Social innovation has also created a variety of initiatives having a strong local dimension: from the regeneration of neighborhoods, to the creation of food networks; from the promotion of local crafts, to strategies to improve the energy self-sufficiency of communities. By inventing and enhancing new socio-cultural and economic activities linked to places, these social innovations have de facto generated a new sense of place and a new idea of locality that we can call *cosmopolitan localism*.

The emerging cosmopolitan localism can thus be seen as an equilibrium between being rooted in a given place and a given community, and being open to global flows of ideas, information, people, things, and money.[19] This is a delicate equilibrium that, obviously, can be easily broken by sliding into a closure towards the outside world, with all of the resulting social and political implications; or into a total opening to what comes from afar, that destroys the specific local characteristics of the social fabric.

To the contrary, when this equilibrium is found and maintained, it creates a new type of place, a place that is no longer an isolated entity, but that becomes a node in a variety of networks: short networks that generate and regenerate the local social and economic fabric, and long networks that connect that particular place, and its community, to the rest of the world.

At the same time, the cosmopolitan localism that social innovation is producing also generates a new idea of well-being, a well-being in which a leading role is played by the recognition of the importance of natural and socio-cultural common goods (such as a lively social fabric, a healthy environment, a nice landscape, and last but not least, the wealth of diversity that a place can express). Translating these observations into project-based terms, we find that places are

not to be considered isolated entities but nodes of short and long-distance networks (with the short networks generating and regenerating the local socio-economic fabric and the long networks connecting a particular community and a particular place to the rest of the world).
The theme of cosmopolitan localism is interwoven with that of distributed systems (see Box 1.3), where the latter can be the technical infrastructure of the former, that which makes it technically possible to realize a world of interconnected places. And where the first is what orients the second: that which gives a cultural, political, and environmental direction to a technical possibility that, otherwise, could go in other, unsustainable directions.[20]

2.7 The double link between functional and relational proximity

How and why the city of diversified proximity is the terrain on which the city of relational proximity can flourish is explained to us by the principle of proximity (which we discussed in Chapter 1), indicating a path that goes from functional to relational proximity: more opportunities for activities in proximity means more likelihood of interaction, encounters, and finding themes and projects to put in common (see Box 1.2).

The observation of reality, and in particular of recent social innovation, tells us, however, that the process can also go in the opposite direction: the more the local communities, the more the local activities and services that they generate in the neighborhood, the more diversified proximity becomes. In short, the richer in community a place is, the more likely it is to have a system of proximity that is in turn rich in services and opportunities.

This double link between the dimensions of proximity, due to which the opportunities for encounters generate relations, and reciprocally, the relations, by becoming project-based, create new opportunities for encounters, could be defined as a *principle of bidirectional proximity*. Its sense is particularly clear in the case of the relationship between social innovation and the scenario we are discussing: we have seen that social innovation is born precisely with the motivation of opening up new opportunities, and that it does so by operating collaboratively on the system of proximity to which it refers (and of which it is a part). By doing so, it increases the offer of the same. In turn, this can generate occasions for new encounters and new conversations, and thus also for new initiatives of social innovation.

In conclusion, the concept of proximity, as it has been proposed here so far, can be useful because it combines, at the local level, the functional dimension and the relational dimension of the systems to which it refers, making it possible to separately discuss the two dimensions, but at the same time showing the double link that connects them and thus allowing for defining the strategies of action based precisely in their reciprocity.

This line of reflection can be connected to that of Richard Sennett, when in his book *Building and Dwelling*,[21] he writes that urban quality depends on interaction, that is more or less dialogic or conflictual, between two of its components: that of the constructed environment (*Ville*) and that of the lived environment (*Cité*). The Ville is seen as a set of material artifacts (houses, streets, squares, and technical infrastructure), while the Cité is considered a maze of interactions, a city consisting of encounters, conversations, and communities; a city whose quality is greater the more encounters and conversations are able to occur, and the more communities have the possibility to emerge.

The description of these two aspects of the city certainly resembles the two dimensions of proximity: the Ville includes the theme of functional proximity, the Cité that of relational proximity. What the introduction of the concept of proximity adds to the interpretation of the city as Ville and as Cité is a project-based indication: to improve the Ville requires the action of the Cité, of its relational proximity and the energy it can generate. And the opposite is true as well: to regenerate the Cité it is necessary to create a richer and more diversified functional proximity in the Ville. As always in the presence of double links, there is no rule that defines once and for all where to start. It needs to be decided on a case-by-case basis. This is where we find the intrinsically project-based and strategic character of this action.

In the last century, modernity viewed the city principally as a constructed city (the Ville), imagining it as a great machine to produce wealth, whose efficiency was given by the existence of specialized zones. Against this reductive vision of reality, already more than fifty years ago, Jane Jacobs began to go against the grain and look at the lived city (the Cité) differently, observing how and to what extent urban quality depended on a complex and unforeseeable combination of diversities: the diversity of people (who could be met there), of events (that could happen there), and of social forms (that could emerge there).[22] This observation had an enormous significance in reorienting the discussion on cities and the practices that derived from it.[23]

However, as Sennett himself points out, Jacobs' proposal had a limit: by concentrating on the lived city, the constructed one appeared as a backdrop whose characteristics seemed not to be in discussion.[24] But as we know all too well, this is not the case. And this is so not only in new cities, where by definition the Ville must be designed and constructed, but also in already-existing cities, in which, by changing over time, it creates conditions that can be more or less favorable for the development of the Cité. In particular, the Ville gives rise to conditions of proximity that can lose their original qualities, reducing their diversity and becoming specialized.

2.8   Encounters, meeting places, and the molecular dimension of the city

Cities are places where strangers can meet.[25] This observation by Richard Sennett can be used to distinguish a city from a pre-modern village. In a city, it is always normal to meet strangers; in a village it is not. But today the sense of this statement must be extended: in a society in which traditional social forms have dissolved, people are increasingly mutual strangers. And thus what Sennet noted extends to everyone, to the point of reaching the definition given by Zygmunt Bauman who says: "A city is a cohabitation of strangers."[26] Thus in contemporary cities we tend to be mutual strangers. But if and when cities function well, they allow us to live together; which means that the intersection of our paths of life can lead to encounters (and not clashes), i.e. to interactions that can evolve into conversations, and thus, in some cases, to new social forms.

However, in order for this to occur, it is necessary for the city to be a city of proximity, and to be so in both its modalities: functional and relational. Only this way, only with this proximity, does it in fact become possible for two mutual strangers to overcome the distances (i.e. the stereotypes and preconceived ideas that operate as spacers) and, discovering on the other hand the elements of closeness (what they can have in common), they exchange something and begin a conversation. All of this requires a favorable environment: there must be a culture of proximity (i.e.

of listening, empathy, and curiosity towards others), but also a suitable space (that allows people to be prepared to listen). On the other hand, we know that, based on the principle of bidirectional proximity we cited, there is a double link between these two dimensions: the culture of proximity depends on places, that is, on the systems of proximity in which they are able to flourish; and vice versa, the existence of places with these qualities requires a culture able to conceive them. Places and culture of proximity, by mutually feeding each other, create a circular process that, depending on each case, can be either positive or negative.

What interests us here is to shed light on how the characteristics of the physical space of the constructed city influence the possibility to generate encounters; and that these encounters can evolve into conversations, and in some cases, into new social forms (where, as stated, encounters, conversations, and social forms are then the construction materials for the lived city). To clarify this point, we must take a very close look at the conditions that make an encounter possible.

Therefore, the question is: how and when do encounters take place that can generate sociality? How and when can a diffused culture of proximity be created?

In order for there to be encounters, people need to find issues of common interest (Bruno Latour would say: a common "matter of concern" must emerge[27]). However, for this to happen, the practical conditions must also be created that make these encounters possible; that allow for communicating with the voice, but also with the eyes and the body. There must be suitable places: the stairway landing for the neighbor, the table of a café for a friend, the street for a stranger. Ultimately, meeting up to exchange ideas, to do something together, or for the simple pleasure of chatting, requires there to be places where two or more people have the possibility to come and stay near to each other, at a distance that allows them to hear, see, and in some cases touch each other. This molecular observation on the proxemics of single encounters tells us something important on a greater scale as well. In order for the city of proximity to be the city of encounters, it must be sufficiently dense to make encounters probable, and sufficiently diversified to offer the possibility to encounter different people while performing different activities. Density and diversity are thus favorable conditions for the generation of encounters, and thus for their possibility to evolve into conversations, and here, in some cases, into the construction of new social forms. Streets, squares, cafés, shops, and public parks are the places where that can take place. It is more difficult for it to take place in the broad empty streets of a neighborhood of single-family homes or isolated blocks.[28]

The density we are speaking of is a thick weave of interactions as they can take place in the streets and squares of an urban form characterized by a particular horizontal density (opposed to the vertical density of cities of isolated skyscrapers and modernist residential blocks); an urban form that, as we have seen in the previous sections discussing the cases of Paris and Barcelona, is not only the most suited to create social quality, but can also easily be oriented towards environmental sustainability. It is an urban form that, obviously, cannot be extended to all cities of the world, but that, given its qualities, could guide the construction of the new cities that are emerging and provide indications for the transformation of existing ones.

Certainly, with the pandemic and the distancing it has imposed, many have rushed to declare the end of the dense city. But this position is based on a misunderstanding: the density we are speaking of does not in fact necessarily imply the formation of gatherings. Furthermore, it seems to have been demonstrated that the places where people reacted best are those in which there was a sufficiently dense and dynamic social fabric to hold up even during the lockdown and the obligation of distancing that ensued.

Box 2.3   Anti-epidemic proxemics

In its original definition, proxemics is the study of how people use and structure space or spatial arrangements in work environments and personal relations (*Collins Dictionary*). Today, the distancing imposed by the pandemic (that is usually defined as "social," but should more properly be called "physical") has produced the need to add to traditional proxemics, defined at the local level by various cultures, a new universal proxemics based on which, for the periods in which it is necessary, a new rule of behavior is imposed: everyone must have a private sphere that, for anti-epidemic reasons, must have a range of no less than three feet. What implications does this new proxemics have for the city? And in particular, what implications does it have for the density and sociality of cities? A response to these questions can be summarized in three points: (1) density does not mean crowding; (2) distancing does not mean social isolation; and (3) distancing does not mean impossibility to collaborate.

Density does not mean crowding. In a situation of anti-epidemic proximity, what must be avoided is crowding (people must not be less than three feet from each other). This has nothing to do with the physical and relational density of a city. Crowding takes place when, for some reason, many people come into contact, or are very close, because there is not enough space to maintain the recommended distances (for example, in a bus or a crowded office); or because we like to be close (such as in a disco, at a party, or at a football game).

Thus, crowding is not linked to urban density, but to the existence or absence of specific reasons that create it. In other words, in a low-density area, the commuter train at rush hour, the bar on Sunday, or the church on certain special occasions can be more crowded than the corresponding places in a densely populated city neighborhood.

Ultimately, distancing does not require low urban density; it requires avoiding situations of crowding.

Distancing does not mean social isolation. Anti-epidemic proximity, per se, does not impede socialization, although it certainly changes the forms in which it can manifest itself. Socialization does not necessarily require contact. There has been much discussion of the strong and weak points of online socialization and the possibility to combine it with offline socialization; that is, with the socialization that, as has always taken place, develops in the physical world. Alongside this discussion, a new one must be added, that regards socialization in the physical world, that takes place though, maintaining the required distance. Social distancing thus leads us to discuss how to promote new forms of hybrid, online-offline socialization, where the offline part takes place interacting in the physical world, but at the proper distance.

Distancing does not prevent collaboration. Anti-epidemic proximity does not prevent collaboration, although it requires new behavior. Furthermore, collaboration allows people to face the required changes in a world that is more acceptable for them – and often also more effective for society. This is the direction taken by a series of collaborative initiatives in the new proxemics. For example, the possibility to mutually help each other, as regards care for the sick, children, and the elderly, and to do so respecting social distancing; or the possibility of a shared, but distant use of neighborhood services, offices in proximity, or games for children, with the precaution of sanitizing the places and objects between uses.

2.9   Local communities, diversified proximity, and resilience

If Jane Jacobs were to walk in her West Village of New York today, or in many other cities that had analogous characteristics at the time, she would not find the qualities that she cherished so much: what at the time was a dense and diversified interweave of relations is losing, or has already lost, its properties. What has happened is that a growing wave of automobiles (with all of their system of parking places, streets, and connections suited for them), tourists (with the related shops and cafés dedicated to them), and above all, real estate speculators (with their plans for commodification of the city) has struck that network, lacerating it and impoverishing it. These elements have separated the rich from the poor, closing each in their own ghetto; reducing the occasions for encounters and reducing the variety of social forms that can be found there; de facto, activating a process of social desertification.

At the same time, the spread of digital technologies, adding to the previous trend and shifting attention from the physical to the digital world, has driven people even farther from the streets and the squares, pushing them towards isolation in their private spaces. This has accelerated the processes of social desertification, with all of their implications in terms of diffused solitude and fragility of the entire urban ecosystem. This is certainly a grave phenomenon, from all points of view, including that of the loss of resilience.

Today – for good reason – there is much talk of resilience. So it is useful to focus briefly on this theme and on the relationship between city, resilience, and proximity.[29] The experiences of the past, and recent experience with Covid-19, tell us that, ultimately, the most resilient cities are those constructed on a web of communities rooted in the places where they live. Observing the behavior of various communities in post-catastrophe conditions has showed that the strongest and best-structured communities have a greater capacity to understand what to do and how to organize themselves after a traumatic event, even when no indications arrive from above.[30] Thus, to give an example, a tennis club can become a rescue center and its members a network of people who know each other well and are able to get organized. There's more: covered courts can become a dormitory; the towels from the showers can be transformed into sheets and bandages; the equipment for the barbeque into a kitchen. In short, the objects used for daily life can be reinterpreted and used in an exceptional moment, functioning as a spontaneous infrastructure for an emergency.[31]

The lesson we can learn here is that after a catastrophic event, when normality and the normal way of doing things collapse, and when communication from the top down doesn't function, people who know each other, and know the places well, can figure out how to get organized and how to use existing resources in the most creative manner; and just as important, by having the necessary relational proximity, they can support each other on a psychological level.

The observations presented to this point have been made on the occasion of earthquakes and hurricanes, but it has been noticed that something similar has also taken place in the case of particularly acute economic and social crises: and the same thing has happened now with the Covid-19 crisis. Thus, to generalize, we can say that the resilience of a city has an important social component: it requires the existence of networks of people who have familiarity with each other in "normal" conditions, and thus, when faced with a crisis, are able to self-organize and face the new problems that arise. In other words, as for social and environmental quality, resilience is greater the more the city presents itself as a complex and vital ecosystem at its molecular scale.

2.10   Streets, squares, common goods, and proximity

A city certainly is not, and cannot be described exclusively based on, how it appears at the molecular level. In order to exist, this level must be based on infrastructures that are necessarily of a greater scale. Furthermore, as we have already observed, its social and cultural life cannot be reduced to the sum of many cases of micro-relations at the neighborhood level. Thus, by introducing the scenario of the city of proximity, we have said that it cultivates the intersection of short networks and long networks, and that ultimately what the scenario proposes is a cosmopolitan localism.

However, we now also know that, while it is true that the quality of a city cannot and must not only be the sum of the qualities of its neighborhoods, it is just as true that there cannot be a resilient and sustainable city, in physical and social terms, without a high quality of its neighborhoods; that is, without a diffused condition of diversified proximity thanks to which there is the possibility and the probability that encounters will be generated, and that they will evolve into conversations, projects, and communities. It is these encounters and conversations, and the social forms that they can generate that, as a whole, when they are present, make the city resilient and produce the political and project-based energies necessary to evolve towards sustainability.

There are various places in which all of this can take place, and others can be invented. But this possibility seems to be expressed the best by the street and the square, understood not as specialized places, i.e. as infrastructure for mobility, but as multifunctional spaces in which different activities and different groups of people co-exist, intersect, and meet in a generative manner, giving rise to conversations and projects. The city of proximity is thus the city of the streets and squares when they function this way.

The problem, unfortunately, is that social desertification is advancing, and the streets and squares function less and less in the manner just described. What can be done to change this trend? The response to this question regards social innovation and the (re)construction of the common goods we spoke of at the beginning of this chapter. The question can therefore be reformulated as follows: how can we promote social innovation and the production of necessary urban common goods? We know that neither one nor the others can be planned directly, but that favorable conditions can be created for their existence. We know that proximity, when it is diversified and well balanced between the functional and the relational components, is the terrain on which to operate.

In doing so, though, we must take into account that what happens in the streets and squares is the physical, local evidence of what takes place in broader networks regarding different themes. More precisely, it is the local interweave of sociotechnical systems which each have their specific logic and modality of functioning. Moreover, we need to take into account that today, these encounters are increasingly the result of something that takes place connecting the digital world with the physical one. So streets and squares can no longer be understood in their functioning outside of their current hybrid, physical-digital dimension.

Lastly, we must learn to think that streets and squares, and the encounters that take place in them, and thanks to them, cannot be separated from being a part of the web of life. Therefore, each square and each street, like each city in which they are located, are elements of a single large complex ecosystem, the Earth.

The answer to the initial question (how to invert the trend of social desertification) thus does not have a simple answer; which was predictable. But this does not mean that there are no possible answers; or, more precisely, that there are no roads to take to find them. We will indicate one in the next chapter, one that is focused on the idea and practice of care, that is based on the assumption that the only antidote to social de-sertification is a renewed capacity for care; and that care, by definition, requires proximity.

Box 2.4   Remote work as a regenerative agent
by *Ivana Pais*

If empty streets and squares represent social desertification, the birth of new places for encounters can be considered a sign of a counter-movement oriented towards the resocialization of our cities. This is what was already happening in the new workplaces starting at the beginning of the new century, that now could undergo an acceleration due to the spread of remote work.

The Eurostat regional yearbook[32] shows us that before the pandemic (in 2019) only 5.5 percent of the EU's workforce aged 20-64 years usually worked from home. This share more than doubled after the Covid-19 pandemic, reaching 12.4 percent in 2020. The most rapid increase was reached in capital and urban regions. The highest share (37 percent) was recorded in the capital region of Finland (Helsinki-Uusimaa), followed by the Province du Brabant Wallon (26.5 percent) and the Région de Bruxelles-Capitale/Brussels Hoofdstedelijk Gewest in Belgium (25.7 percent), Eastern and Midland Region in Ireland (24.7 percent), Wien in Austria (24.2 percent), Hovedstaden in Denmark (23.6 percent) and Île-de-France in France (23.4 percent). Working from home was less prevalent across many of the eastern and southern regions of the EU; less than 5.0 percent in Croatia, Cyprus, Latvia, Bulgaria, Romania and the majority of the regions in Greece. Workers employed in professional, financial, information and communication, education and government sectors had greater home working opportunities, while there were fewer opportunities for people employed in manual occupations within the agriculture, manufacturing and distributive trades sectors. Emergency home working allowed for maintaining operations for a significant share of businesses and maintaining the jobs of millions of workers. At the same time, it led to experimenting with alternative forms of organization of work. Starting with Twitter – with a cascade effect especially in high-tech companies – numerous companies stated that now workers will always be able to choose their place of work. And the idea of introducing forms of hybrid remote working is even more widespread. It is certainly early to make predictions and understand how these announcements will translate into organizational practices, but the direction seems to be clear, and It Is useful to reflect on the relevant implications. Teleworkability – measured as the share of jobs that can potentially be performed at home – is estimated around one third of occupations in G-7 countries,[33] with higher shares in more urban regions.

The prospect of a spread of remote working shifts strategies that until now have regarded businesses, to the level of the single worker. While until now delocalization has regarded companies that transfer production from their national territory to other countries where labor costs are lower, now the issue is to leave the work facility the same but have the possibility to place their workers (at least in part) in new work premises. This happens in a phase in which, among other things, companies are implementing reshoring strategies.

This perspective represents a challenge for the city of proximity, because it leads to considering citizens not only as consumers or users of services, but also their dimension as workers and producers. While infrastructure such as railroads has allowed for the mobility of objects and persons and has extended the borders of cities because it has allowed for commuting, the new platforms based on cloud logics allow people to remain where they are and work on digital objects shared with people who are far away.

While on the one hand the possibility of an increase of the flexibility of employees' work hours and spaces generates certain worries linked to the generalization of project-based work, with a consequent fragmentation of work activities, on the other it leads to looking at the solutions implemented in recent years by self-employed professionals to face the risks linked to similar methods of governing work. Among these solutions, in the discussion of the city of proximity, new workplaces play a central role; not only coworking spaces, but more in general, those that have been defined as smart working places:[34] cafés, restaurants, and hotels that equip their spaces to host workers. For self-employed professionals, those places have represented indispensable social infrastructure to maintain relational and professional roots in an increasingly fragmented labor market.

The spread of emergency remote work led coworking spaces to be reorganized to host coworkers with different characteristics and needs: not only self-employed but also employees and companies. During the pandemic emergency, employees rented workstations to have a safe place to work outside of the home. An interesting case is that of the parents who used workstations on a rotating basis, alternating their responsibilities of care. Among businesses, we see a shift from startups that rented coworking workstations and offices in anticipation of growing and moving to an independent office, and companies in crisis that used coworking following downsizing operations.

It should also be noted that, during the pandemic emergency, spaces in city centers suffered more than others, while those in areas outside of urban centers filled up again rapidly, precisely because they are located in residential neighborhoods. This strengthens the proposal of a polycentric city, where each zone has the tools to develop as an autonomous center of social, cultural, and economic life. But in order for this to happen, adequate urban policies are needed that favor the accessibility and vitality of more peripheral neighborhoods.

The most interesting aspect with respect to the questions at issue in this book, though, is the emergence of proximity coworking. While in the past shared workspaces were selected by the coworkers based on professional specialization (coworking linked to the digital sector, the world of art, the film industry, etc.) or as a function of the services offered, now a new workspace is emerging that presents itself as a point of reference for a local community. Proximity coworking is not only a workspace dedicated to workers who reside in the same neighborhood, but often it is proposed as a multiservice hub in favor of the local territory, making available the professional skills of the coworkers, as well as services of a cultural nature (for events, shows, etc.) and a social nature (assistance for children and youth, reception services, etc.).

In a situation where work is increasingly scattered, fragmented, and digital, these places can reaggregate people, interests, and ideas. They can transform a residential area into a more or less structured local community, and potentially, its inhabitants into collective actors. It is also evident that this dynamic can also generate new tensions at the local level, linked to new forms of inequality and segregation (between areas and workers), and as such require an intentional project-based investment and the search for new forms of governance at the local level.

Notes

[1] E. Ostrom, *Governing the Commons. The Evolution of Institutions for Collective Action*, Cambridge, Cambridge University Press, 1990 (Italian trans. *Governare i beni collettivi*, Venice, Marsilio, 2006).

[2] Michel Bauwens, "Towards the Partner State Model of Commons Governance," https://blog.p2pfoundation.net/, September 2012; Gregorio Arena, Christian Iaione, *L'età della condivisione. La collaborazione tra cittadini e amministrazione per i beni comuni*, Rome, Carocci Editore, 2015.

[3] C. Donolo, "I beni comuni presi sul serio," www.labsus.org, 2017.

[4] EVStudio AEP, "The Neighborhood Unit: How Does Perry's Concept Apply to Modern Day Planning?" https://evstudio.com/, May 30, 2019.

[5] C40 is a coalition for the climate of 97 of the largest cities in the world, that at the local level, aim to reach more ambitious goals than those of the Paris Agreement. They represent over 700 million citizens and one-fourth of the global economy. Recently, C40 posed the idea of the 15-minute city as a model for post-Covid economic recovery. See: https://www.c40.org/about.

[6] C40 Cities Climate Leadership Group, C40 Knowledge Hub, "How to build back better with a 15-minute city," https://www.c40knowledgehub.org/.

[7] Semaest, as the company is named, intervenes in Paris and the region, and is specialized in the revitalization of artisanship and commerce through the promotion of a new neighborhood economy. See www.semaest.fr.

[8] Ibid.

[9] Carlos Moreno, "The 15 minutes-city: for a new chrono-urbanism!," http://www.moreno-web.net/, June 30, 2019; Idem, *Urban life and proximity at the time of covid-19*, Paris, Editions de l'Observatoire, 2020; Idem, *Droit de cité, de la "ville-monde" à la "ville du quart d'heure,"* Paris, Éditions de l'Observatoire, 2020.

[10] Cited in David Roberts, "Barcelona's Superblocks Are a New Model for 'Post-Car' Urban Living," https://www.vox.com/, April 11, 2019.

[11] Press release of the City of Barcelona, November 11, 2020 (Ajuntament de Barcelona, *Cap a la Superilla Barcelona*, https://ajuntament.barcelona.cat).

[12] "Decidim helps citizens, organizations and public institutions self-organize democratically at every scale" (https://decidim.org).

[13] BCNecologia, *Charter for the Ecositemic Planning of the Cities and the Metropolies*, https://charterbcnecologia.wordpress.com/.

[14] Salvador Rueda, "L'ecologia urbana i la planificación de la ciutat," *Medi Ambient Tecnologia i Cultura*, 5, 1993, *Repensar la ciutat*, pp. 6-17; Salvador Rueda, Rafael de Cáceres, Albert Cuchí, Lluís Brau, *El Urbanismo Ecologico*, Barcelona, BCNecologia (Agencia de Ecologia Urbana), 2012.

[15] Domenico De Masi, *Smart Working. La rivoluzione del lavoro intelligente*, Venice, Marsilio, 2020, p. 14.

[16] Wolfgang Sachs (ed.), *The Development Dictionary. A Guide to Knowledge as Power*, London, Zed Books, 1992 (Italian trans. *Dizionario dello sviluppo*, It. ed. edited by A. Tarozzi, Torino Edizioni Gruppo Abele, 1998); Idem, *Planet Dialectics. Exploration in Environment and Development*, London, Zed Books, 1999 (Italian trans. *Ambiente e giustizia sociale. I limiti della globalizzazione*, presentation and editing by G. Onufrio, Rome, Editori riuniti, 2002); Ezio Manzini, "Small, Local, Open and Connected: Design Research Topics in the Age of Networks and Sustainability," *Journal of Design Strategies*, 4(1), Spring 2010; Manzini, M'Rithaa, "Distributed systems and cosmopolitan localism," cit.

[17] David Harvey, *The Condition of Postmodernity. An Enquiry into the Origins of Cultural Change*, Oxford, Blackwell, 1990 (Italian trans. *La crisi della modernità*, Milan, Il Saggiatore, 1993); Zygmunt Bauman, *La società dell'incertezza*, Bologna, Il Mulino, 1999; Ulrich Beck, *Was ist Globalisierung? Irrtümer des Globalismus – Antworten auf Globalisierung*, Frankfurt, Suhrkamp, 1997 (Italian trans. *Che cos'è la globalizzazione. Rischi e prospettive della società planetaria*, Rome, Carocci, 1999).

[18] George Ritzer, *The McDonaldization of society*, Rev. new century ed., Thousand Oaks, Pine Forge Press, 2004 (first ed. 1997; Italian trans. *Il mondo alla McDonald's*, Bologna, Il Mulino, 1997).

[19] Arjun Appadurai, "Disgiunzione e differenza nell'economia culturale globale," in M. Featherstone, *Cultura globale. Nazionalismo, globalizzazione e modernità*, Rome, Seam, 1990.

[20] Manzini, M'Rithaa, "Distributed systems and cosmopolitan localism," cit.; Escobar, *Designs for the Pluriverse*, cit.; Terry Irwin, "Transition Design: A Proposal for a New Area of Design Practice, Study, and Research," Design and Culture, 7(2), 2015, pp. 229-246; Gideon Kossoff, *Cosmopolitan Localism: The Planetary Networking of Everyday Life in Place, Cuaderno Journal* 73 (Transition Design Monograph), 2019; Alexandros Schismenos, Vasilis Niaros, Lucas Lemos, "Cosmolocalism: Understanding the Transitional Dynamics Towards

Post-Capitalism," *tripleC: Communication, Capitalism & Critique*, September 21, 2020, pp. 670-684.

[21] Richard Sennett, *Building and Dwelling: Ethics for the City*, New York, Farrar Strauss & Giroux, 2018 (Italian trans. *Costruire e abitare*, Milan, Feltrinelli, 2020).

[22] Jane Jacobs, *The Death and Life of the Great American City*, New York, Vintage, 1992 (first ed. 1961; Italian trans. *Vita e morte delle grandi città. Saggio sulle metropoli americane*, Turin, Einaudi, 1969).

[23] Similar opinions have been expressed not only by Richard Sennet, as already mentioned, but by other careful observers of cities: from Henri Lefebvre to Charles Landry and David Harvey. Starting from different points of view and using different words, they also appreciated the fact that the city was the place where it was possible and probable that multiple encounters would take place. Henri Lefebvre, *Le Droit à la ville*, Paris, Anthropos, 1968 (Italian trans. *Il diritto alla città*, Venice, Marsilio, 1970); Charles Landry, *The Art of City Making*, London, Earthscan, 2006 (Italian trans. *City making. L'arte di fare la città*, ed. it. edited by M. Raino, Turin, Codice, 2009); David Harvey, *Rebel Cities: From the Right to the City to the Urban Revolution*, London, Verso Books, 2012 (Italian trans. *Città ribelli. I movimenti urbani dalla Comune di Parigi a Occupy Wall Street*, Milan, Il Saggiatore, 2013).

[24] Sennett, *Costruire e abitare*, cit.

[25] Richard Sennett, "A flexible city of strangers," https://mondediplo.com/, February 2001.

[26] Zygmunt Bauman, *City of Fears, City of Hopes*, London, Goldsmiths College, 2003, p. 5 (Italian trans. *Città di paure, città di speranze*, Rome, Castelvecchi, 2018).

[27] Bruno Latour, "Why Has Critique Run Out of Steam? From Matters of Fact to Matters of Concern," *Critical Inquiry*, 30(2), 2004, pp. 225-248.

[28] Jan Gehl, *Cities for People*, Washington, Island Press, 2010 (Italian trans. *Città per le persone*, Santarcangelo di Romagna, Maggioli, 2017); Idem, *Life Between Buildings*, Washington, Island Press, 2011.

[29] Ezio Manzini, Adam Thorpe, "Weaving People and Places: Art and Design for Resilient Communitues," *She Ji: The Journal of Design, Economics, and Innovation*, 4, i, Spring 2018.

[30] Robert J. Sampson, *Great American City: Chicago and the Enduring Neighborhood Effect*, Chicago, The University of Chicago Press, 2012.

[31] Adam Greenfield, "Practices of the Minimum Viable Utopia," *Architectural Design*, 87(1), 2017, pp. 16-25.

[32] The *Eurostat Regional Yearbook – 2021 Edition* can be viewed and downloaded from https://doi.org/10.2785/894358.

[33] OECD, *Implications of Remote Working Adoption on Place Based Policies: A Focus on G7 Countries*, Paris, OECD Publishing, 2021, DOI: 10.1787/b12f6b85-en.

[34] For further discussion, we refer to the study *Smart Workers e Smart Working Places: lavorare oltre l'ufficio* produced by Percorsi di Secondo Welfare and Centro di Ricerca e Documentazione Luigi Einaudi (available at https://innova.srl/landing-page-smart-working/).

3   The City that Cares

"It takes a village to raise a child." Thus says an African proverb, and that's how it was in the past for us, too. The sense of this proverb can be extended: it takes a village – or a neighborhood – also to take care of an elderly person, or someone who is particularly fragile. Ultimately, it takes a village to have a society capable of mutual care. The proverb speaks of a strong connection between activities of care and the village, understood as both a community and a physical place: to provide care the way the proverb tells us, physical closeness goes hand in hand with relational closeness. In the village everyone is around the others, in all senses. The village that cares is that of proximity, with the wealth of meanings we have discussed.

But the village is no longer. With it, the community and proximity of the village have left us, along with the possibility of that exact type of care. For all of this, for this proximity, community, and care, we can be nostalgic, or not. In any event, they will not return in that form. However, faced with the multiple crises we are now in, we can look back at the village – but also at premodern cities – to seek ideas on how to emerge from the difficulties we are in. In the previous chapters we assumed that an idea on which to work was proximity, in its dual functional and relational dimensions, and its possibility to qualify the relationship between places and community. In the previous chapter, we saw that modernity, generating increasingly functional and specialized proximity, produced the city of distances, with all that implies in social and environmental terms. But we have also seen that it is possible to modify this tendency; that social innovation tells us where to go and that it is possible to go there; and that technical innovation, that has led to the city of distances, can sustain the city of proximity.

We will continue down this path here, discussing the relationship between proximity and care. At the center of the discussion will be the recognition that the city of proximity is the city of care. Or more precisely, it is the *city that cares*:[1] an ecosystem of people, organizations, places, products and services that, as a whole, express a mutual capacity for care.

The starting point is obviously a reflection on the very concept of care, that brings into focus a fundamental aspect for us: there is no care without contact, and thus without proximity. Thus the city of distances produced by modernity is intrinsically a careless city; and thus, the physical/digital hybridization of proximity intersects with the analogous hybridization of care. So when social innovation proposes new care services, it also tells us a lot about what the city of proximity could be like and how it could function.

3.1   Care and proximity / Care is proximity

Care is "a species activity that includes everything that we do to maintain, continue, and repair our 'world' so that we can live in it as well as possible. That world includes our bodies, ourselves, and our environment."[2] Defined as such more than thirty years ago by Joan Tronto and Berenice Fischer, the idea of care refers to the entire web of interactions between humans that compose the social fabric. But that is not all: is also extends towards "the world," i.e. everything that is interdependent in the web of life. In practical terms, what all practices of care share is the responsibility to support, repair, and maintain life in the broader ecosystem of which they are a part; an action that requires a responsible attitude on the part of everyone, and that, for this reason, cannot be produced by someone singularly but must be generated in a process of co-production that involves multiple interdependent entities.

Proceeding with this line of thinking, Maria Puig de la Bellacasa, in her book *Matters of Care*,[3] brings into focus two themes that are particularly useful for the purpose of our reflection on proximity: that of tactility and that of sociality.[4] Care, writes de la Bellacasa, has an unavoidable tactile dimension: to have care, there must be contact. When we touch, we are also touched; when we care, we are also cared for. Care thus implies a sense of closeness and reciprocity. This observation brings us directly to the theme we are discussing: care requires proximity, relational and functional proximity. A city of distances is also a careless city. This is in fact what has happened, unfortunately, and what we should learn to combat.

The idea and practices of care and proximity that we can seek today are certainly different than those of the African village cited at the beginning of this chapter, but also than those of the neighborhood from the last century. In Chapter 2, we discussed this as regards proximity. Here we will look at it as regards care, noting that the two terms, care and proximity, coevolve maintaining their close interaction. There is no care without proximity; and there is no proximity without care. Of course, as we have seen, proximity can become hybrid, and as we will see, this can happen for care. But in both cases, in order for proximity and care to truly remain as such, there must be a physical dimension in which one body is physically close to another one.

The theme of reciprocity, however, brings us to that of sociality. We have said that care is not to be considered an action, but an interaction: we touch and are touched. We care and are cared for. But if we consider the child whom the village cares for, or if we consider the elderly or sick who need care in a city, this reciprocity is not directly visible. Once again, de la Bellacasa comes to the rescue, saying that "the reciprocity of care is rarely bilateral: the living tissue of care is not maintained thanks to individuals who give and receive a counterparty, but thanks to a diffused collective effort."[5] In other words, care must not be understood as the action of someone towards another person or object at a specific moment, but as the different ways it presents itself, or could present itself, in a society: we have all been children, and we will all become old (if we don't die first), many of us will have children and we will all have sicknesses. Thus we all have had, and will have, a need for care. All of us, when we act with attention and empathy towards others and towards the world, create relationships of care. If the society and the city do not see themselves this way, it is not possible to recognize the social dimension and characteristic of care.

To the contrary of what dominant thinking leads us to believe today, care is not an individual action to be carried out merely between someone who has a need and someone who offers solutions. This way of seeing things is the result of an approach that places care at the center of a process of individualization of people and that imagines society as a sum of healthy and productive individuals, who must compete and do not have time to lose (and who therefore, in this way of seeing things, do not have time and attention to dedicate to care). When you are not like this, not competitive, either you are repaired (if possible), or discarded (if you cannot be repaired).

This idea of care as a precise solution to individual problems has dominated the last half-century, and has accompanied the way in which the idea of service and that of welfare have developed. Now, more than half a century later, it is clear that this way of seeing things has led us to a situation of crisis. And Covid-19 has made this crisis even more evident, although in a paradoxical manner. Precisely at the time in which we are asked to maintain distances, the new condition of life that the pandemic has imposed shows everyone, tangibly, the importance of proximity, both in relational terms and functional terms; both at the molecular level, in the solution of daily problems, and in the sense of closeness that this can provide, and on a large scale; both in the physical world and the hybrid world (forcing us to find ways to be close and in contact even without touching each other).[6]

Box 3.1   Being in contact without contact

Covid-19 has imposed on the world (also) a great social experiment: how to live with physical separation, how to develop a proxemics of life at not-less-than-three-feet-away. This experiment has led to developing new forms of micro-sociality and care: there are those who have helped the elderly, the local shops that have delivered products to homes, and the neighborhood bookstores that have sponsored cultural activities. But in any case, the way in which someone has taken care of someone else, has stopped at the front door of the house, or in any event, at least three feet away.

This observation leads us to reconsider the tactile dimension of care, as proposed to us by de la Bellacasa. In fact, the examples shown here tell us of care without contact, and the shopping bags left by a friend or a volunteer in front of the door are the paradigmatic example.[7]

De la Bellacasa introduces the relationship between care and tactility because the sense of touch is that with the clearest reciprocity (I can see without being seen, or hear without being heard, but I can't touch without being touched). Thus it is the sense that best expresses the interdependence that connects all of the entities that have a role in a relationship of care.

The micro-sociality that the pandemic has forced us to invent shows us, though, that what truly counts is not so much physical tactility, but proximity intended as a sense of closeness that in some cases, such as those proposed, can even take place without direct contact: care that is proposed as being in contact without contact. In order for this to happen, though, the interlocutors must be in a condition of physical and relational proximity. Concretely, it is necessary for them to know each other and live in close proximity. Indeed, it is not the same if the person who leaves the bag of groceries in front of the door is a friend, a neighbor, or someone from the corner store, or if it is an unknown person, and we don't know where they come from.

The theme of care without contact is thus closely linked to that of proximity: interaction without contact can be defined as care only if the actors involved are in proximity. If they know each other, there is continuity of interaction. When these conditions are given the practical value of mutual aid, it is combined with the psychological value of feeling the presence of the other and the sense of care. This is also true when, for some reason, there is contact without contact.

3.2   Care is also care work

In daily language, care recalls various meanings. We will list three here.

The first (that we will call *care/1*) refers to *dedicating attention* to someone or something. This is linked to the definition we started with, the reflections that ensued, and the vision of the city of proximity as the caring city.

The second meaning (that we will call *care/2*) is more specific, and regards situations in which attention becomes *taking responsibility* for someone or something. So the emphasis goes on the actions to carry out in regard to people or objects that have needs, because they are sick, or because they are not independent, such as children or the elderly, or because, if we refer to objects, they are particularly fragile or require maintenance. In this case, the interaction of care requires a demanding and recognizable commitment as a true *work of care*: an activity that is not always formally recognized and remunerated, but that can be defined through the specific skills and duties of which it consists. In principle, this second meaning should be included in the first: everything that requires care (intended as care/2) should be done with care (intended as care/1); although we know that often this is not the case: care work is often not done with care.

Lastly, there is a third meaning (that we will call *care/3*) in which care is the synonym of *therapy*, and as the dictionary says, "[care] refers to the set of therapeutic means and medical prescriptions that have the aim of healing a sickness."[8] So normally, it is the result of care work: the caring person prescribes the care to the cared-for person. But this same meaning could be extended to care/1: faced with a society in crisis and a sick planet, it is necessary to find a care/3, understood as therapy, such as the indications to follow to heal; like a set of strategies and policies to re-spin the web of life.[9]

Speaking of the city that cares, the term is certainly to be understood in the sense of care/1, i.e. the meaning closest to the general definition we started from. In this chapter, though, to give more tangible form to the concrete nature of the arguments we will present, the examples will refer principally to care/2, inasmuch as it is more visible and measurable as true care work. We will do it considering care/2 as one of the ways of presenting care/1. This, not only for a reason of principle (because this is how it should be), but also for two very practical reasons, related to each other. The first is that it is increasingly difficult to draw a clear line of demarcation between who and what needs care/2 and who does not (i.e. between the sick and the healthy, or between what is and is not to be "treated with care"). The second is that the separation between care/1 and care/2, and the transformation of the latter into a system of professionalized services without care, is one of the reasons for the social and environmental crisis we are experiencing. We are in fact seeing that there cannot be a society, and a city, of services without care/1; and thus, for the reasons we have stated, without proximity.

Discussing care/2, i.e. care work, thus implies speaking of time, attention, energy, capability, and the skills it requires. This necessarily means dealing with its distribution in society and the inequalities in the midst of which it takes place; which therefore include those based on gender disparity. In fact, everything that can be said about the distribution of care work cannot avoid the fact that the burden of that work has always fallen – and still falls – largely on the shoulders of women. The theme of redistribution of care work (that as we will see, is one of the terrains on which to operate to approach the city of proximity) therefore must be developed so as to guarantee that this gender disparity will be overcome; that as we can observe daily, clashes with all types of blocks.

That said, we can see how we came to the current situation of crisis, that regards care/1 but appears and manifests itself above all as a crisis of care/2. To do this, we will summarize some fundamental steps in the evolution of care/2, i.e. of care work.

From the start of human history, care and care work have been exchanged (given and received) within groups that are culturally homogenous, durable, and relatively closed: families, clans, village communities, and urban neighborhoods (in all of these cases, most of the care work was the responsibility of women). More recently, with an acceleration in the last two centuries, care has also been practiced by dedicated services: hospitals, pre-schools, nursing homes (in this case as well, most of the care work was and is done by women, often in unstable working conditions or with low salaries). For these systems of services, in the last century the idea of reference became that of industrialization of care; a scenario in which the services had to be organized with criteria of efficiency similar to that of the Fordist factory of that period.

Today, for various reasons (which we will come back to later), the demand for care/2 is growing and becoming more complex, while both the informal and formal offer of that care is becoming less and less able to satisfy the demand. In fact, in the current fluid and hyper-individualized societies, families and villages and neighborhood communities are becoming weaker (if not entirely disappearing) and individuals, given the way they are led to structure their daily lives, have fewer and fewer practical possibilities to take care of others (even when, in principle, they would like to do so). In turn, service systems, that in the scenario of industrialized care were supposed to substitute the practices of traditional care, have less and less capacity to do so, because they don't have enough financial resources (and often political will), but also, and above all, because the idea of service on which they are based is unable to deal with the dimension and variety of the problems they should address.

The distance between this growing demand for care and the contracting supply is at the base of the current crisis of care. Starting here, different scenarios appear, that not coincidentally, can be described in parallel with those that we have seen when speaking of proximity: the scenario of online care (that corresponds to the city of everything at/from home) and the scenario of collaborative care (that obviously corresponds to the city of proximity).

The first of the two, the scenario of online care, has in its favor all of the strong points we have seen introducing the scenario of anything at/from home, with the entirely dystopian characteristics – in our view – that distinguish it; and that in this case, are given by the prospect of the spread of teleassistance that in reality becomes teleabandonment: people left at home in total solitude, but with remote medical monitoring. Then there is the addition that, given the necessary tactile dimension of care, teleassistance services should also be supplemented by the presence in the home of robots that function as nurses and caregivers, and provide company. This scenario takes to the extreme the consequences of the idea of a society and a city of atomized individuals, closed in their private spaces, under the control of sociotechnical systems over which they are unable to exercise any control (while they are constantly controlled by them, though). To be clear: teleassistance, and in some cases, even domestic robots, can be used in a useful and socially valid way, but this can take place only if they are part of solutions of proximity; that is, only if they support activity with the physical presence of people.

The second scenario, that of collaborative care, converges with the scenario of the city of proximity and has the same prerogatives: it is a scenario that goes against the currently dominant trends and practices, but we find it anticipated in the results of many social innovations. This scenario gives us a clear indication of how care work should be distributed. It in fact offers us the vision of an urban ecosystem in which the work of care is distributed fairly among a very large number of people. In the past, this took place as a result of traditional urban forms and types of action. To obtain a similar distribution today (but one that is also fair in gender terms), it is necessary to think of and implement projects, upon defining certain rules, and creating enabling platforms on which the collaborative services operate. This is what we will discuss in the next section.

Box 3.2   The nature of care work

There are many activities that come under care work: some can be carried out by anyone willing to do them (such as taking care of shopping for someone who is momentarily sick); others require more time, attention, and assumption of responsibility (such as taking care of the daily needs of a seriously ill person); still others can require timely interventions by highly specialized experts (such as surgery).

In general terms, these different activities are characterized by a set of parameters such as: time (duration, frequency, and flexibility); skills (normal abilities of daily life, specific but widespread knowledge, and specialist knowledge); responsibility (very low, low, high, very high). Care work should thus be characterized and mapped out using parameters of this type. Their different combination corresponds to different profiles of care work, and thus to the different people who can perform them.

Currently, care work involves a mix of three principal resources: health care operators (specialized and professionals); third sector and charity organizations (specialized and non-specialized, professionals and non-professionals); and traditional communities of care (families, village communities, and urban neighborhoods). We know that, for various reasons, all three of these social resources have a hard time dealing with growing demand. Thus, there is a need to redefine the system of service, and more in general to transform the ecosystem of care to facilitate the emergence of new resources.

Where can these new resources be found? In an involvement of a larger number of people in care activities, given that, as we have said, most care work does not require specialist skills. The problem, though, is that all care work requires time and attention; and time and attention are widespread but limited (each person has a limit to their ability to dedicate attention and the time they can do so). That is not all: we live in a society in which we are pushed to think we don't have time and we are unable to pay attention. So the redefinition of the service system that becomes necessary must find a way to enable people with limited time and attention to provide care. At the same time, it must generate a new culture of time and attention, and thus of care.

3.3   Careless cities

Once upon a time, children could play in the street, by themselves. Nobody was in charge of organizing them and checking what they were doing, but in reality many people did just that: the shopkeeper, the three pensioners on the bench, a person at the window. Each of them knew those children because they lived around there. So they kept their eye on them, and if it became necessary, they intervened.

What has been described here is not a service in the current, economic sense of the term; there is not one person who receives something tangible and another who provides it. It does not have a cost: it uses a common good consisting of that public place (the street), plus the interplay of relations of trust of those who live there. It is not produced by an individual person, but is generated by a heterogeneous sum of factors: a public place, the relations between people, an ethic of collaboration, and mutual aid that has been built up and shared over time. The result is a common good, a neighborhood that cares.

For a long time this common good, like every other common good, was not recognized for its value and importance. Then, like every other common good, it was sacrificed on the altar of progress. And today we are paying the consequences. What happened? Why?

Let us stick with the emblematic example of the children who played in the street, and who today, except for with rare exceptions, no longer do so. The first thing that jumps out is that in the streets and squares, instead of children, there are usually cars. But this is certainly not all: even where there are no cars, it is difficult to find children who play in the street; that dense fabric of relations and trust that made it possible for there to be a web of neighborhood security around them has been lost. Therefore, in these conditions, it is thought – not without reason – that it is not safe to leave children to play alone in the street.[10] So here we are, with streets full of cars and children closed in their homes glued to their videogames or television sets. The more fortunate ones are transported by stressed parents to places where services of sociality and activities for children are offered; from the playground to the language course, to the gym. We have gone from the neighborhood that cares to the city of services; services for the "care" of children, in this example. But the example, as we were saying, is emblematic of a more general reality.

In fact, to generalize, it appears that the city capable of care from the past, which was the expression of a social capital accumulated over time, has been replaced by the city of services (to be precise, we should say: by a possible interpretation of the service society, but we will come back to this later), with all of the worrying implications that have derived therefrom.

A quarter century ago, John McKnight had already rung the alarm and criticized the service society, as it was emerging at the time, speaking of a *careless society*.[11] This author's criticism started from a qualitative observation: social and medical services and the justice system intervene also in areas where they should not. When this happens, according to McKnight, what was supposed to be assistance for people becomes control over people, and what was supposed to be care becomes a commercial activity. The result is the zeroing of the role of the community and the capacity for mutual care by citizens. In brief: the city of services transformed citizens into customers. Given this situation, what McKnight proposed was a generalized deregulation: people and communities must be free to act, and find the most suitable solutions by themselves.

These conclusions, and their social and political implications, must be discussed, and we will do so later. But after twenty-five years we can certainly say that the analytic part of his work was and is more than correct. The service society to which McKnight refers, by transforming citizens into customers, does not function and cannot function; in qualitative terms because it generates a careless society; and in quantitative terms because, if for each human being every demand for care is transformed into a need to be satisfied with a service, there will never be the resources necessary to give everyone the services that would become necessary, regarding everything.

To take a step forward on this theme, we will draw on help from Hilary Cottam, a researcher, designer, and social entrepreneur, whose observations, referring principally to English welfare, highlight broader themes: that is, the roots of the way of doing and thinking that led to the crisis of the welfare system that we have known in Europe until now. In essence, Cottam's critique, as it appears in her latest book *Radical Help*,[12] is this: the welfare system, and in general the idea of the service society that supports it, are in crisis because the model on which they were constructed is currently unsuitable to function. The crisis of the welfare system that we see today has various causes. The most evident shows us the disasters caused by privatization and public spending cuts, with the dramatic increase of social and gender inequality. But a deeper reason (and this is the one Cottam concentrates on) lies in the fact that we have reached the limits of what could be done with a conception of services such as the one that took hold in the post-war period: services as specific individual solutions to specific individual problems,[13] a way to see them that had been conceived and realized for a society that no longer exists. The aging of the population and its implications in medical and social terms are the most obvious demonstration: if being old is considered only a set of problems to solve and diseases to treat, the increase of the demand for services becomes such that there can be no health care system, as understood to this point, that is able to face it. Analogous considerations can be made in reference to the spread of chronic diseases and food disorders. Similarly, no social service conceived to intervene on people in specific moments of difficulty can properly face a situation in which, for a growing number of people, precariousness tends to become the normal condition of existence;[14] with all of the individual and social implications that entails.

The critique of this model of welfare and the corresponding system of services has a long history by now. But for many years, although the problems increased and it became increasingly difficult not to see them, it remained a minority position. Then 2020 came, and everything changed. On this theme as well, Covid-19 forced everyone to see what they previously didn't want to see. As László Herczeg and Lekshmy Parameswaran write about The Care Lab, "The early signs that our Systems of Care – healthcare, eldercare and social care – were vulnerable and fragile had been there; the fissures and cracks were forming steadily over the years" but now Covid-19 has made them visible and tangible for everyone, showing that "when we're not able to deliver Care, when the System crumbles and puts hundreds of thousands of lives at risk, the only thing we can do – all of us – is to stop and stay at home."[15]

The pandemic crisis thus made it evident and tangible for everyone that it is necessary to redesign the system of care so as to have a social, detailed, and inclusive coverage of the territory; that it is necessary to imagine welfare that is collaborative and characterized by proximity. This means redefining the service society as a society in which services are collaborative and distributed throughout the territory, with the task of stimulating and enabling all of the available social resources, starting with those of the people directly involved; services that support new communities and new forms of proximity, the community of care and the proximity that cares.

3.4   Services that help collaborate

The city that cares, the way it was in the past, cannot come back. The care that we can hypothesize for the future cannot ignore the way things have developed in the meantime: the technologies we have produced and how they have changed us, for better and for worse. The thesis proposed here is that the idea of the city that cares can be revived and contextualized in today's world; and that to do so, we need to update the idea of service. To be more precise: we need to shift from the service society that we knew to a society in which services, instead of pushing people to feel and act like passive customers, support their ability to be active, to collaborate, to produce common goods and care for each other and the planet. To address this issue, we must first make a digression on services and their possible different ways of being posed.

In current language, when we speak of services we refer to sociotechnical systems that are more or less large and complex: from the shop on the street to the hypermarket, from the taxi cooperative to the state railway company, from the caregiver to the national health service.[16] What is generally not noticed is that at the heart of each of these there are always one or more encounters in which the interlocutors begin a conversation on what is to be done; that is, on something they intend to do together to reach a result. These encounters, *service encounters*, therefore characterize the quality of the entire service (that, understood as a sociotechnical organization, can include not only these service encounters, but also a variety of other different activities).

This could be a formal definition: a service encounter is an interaction (between people and between people and objects) that, by utilizing a given set of resources (physical and social), reaches a result in which all of the participants recognize a value (a result, that is, that leads to solving a problem or giving access to a new opportunity).

It should be noted, and stressed, that when looking at things this way, service encounters are not only formalized encounters (in public and private services), but also those that take place informally (for example, within a family or a community). To be clear: service encounters are those we can have with a bank employee, a waiter in a café, an unauthorized parking attendant, or a neighbor who has been so kind as to look after our cat while we were away. Today, service encounters are also those we have online with the employee of a call service. It's harder to say whether, and to what extent, contact with an automatic answering service or Amazon's voice assistant Alexa are service encounters. If we leave the discussion on this latter point open, the fact remains that, with the definition proposed, it appears clear that the services have always existed, but have taken different forms. It should be added that this definition of service encounter does not include encounters that take place in conditions of servitude,[17] a term that denotes an interaction in which some have complete power over others, and the latter are obliged to follow orders; this is an interaction in which there is no sharing of the value of the result to be reached (while in our definition, this value sharing is a defining aspect of service interactions when properly considered).[18] Obviously, however clear the difference between service and servitude is in principle, and as important as it is to understand, in practice, the boundary between the two is not so clear. And there can be services in which the power differential between the interlocutors is so strong as to make them become, de facto, forms of servitude.

Concentrating now on formalized service encounters, we can observe that traditionally they have been, and still are, constructed on a strong asymmetry between the actors, i.e. between those who provide and those who receive the service, with the latter, who receive it, placed in the role of customers. In characterizing them, we can add two more elements to this first provider-customer polarity: that of expert-inexpert and that of active-passive. Over time, the evolution of services based on this form of interaction has taken place finding various forms of equilibrium within the three polarities. In the last century, in the name of user-friendliness, they have been designed to be easier and easier to use. This, per se, is certainly not to be criticized. But, if we expand the horizon and see how these types of services have gradually replaced informal services and the ability to do things yourself, what we see is a growing number of people pushed into the position of customers, who are passive and lack skills (to the point of losing the most elementary skills related to daily life: from preparing food to dealing with minor indispositions). In other words, overall, these services can be seen as agents of a vast process of *social disabling*.[19]

Parallel to this, in the name of efficiency, these same services have tended to be standardized, and as we already mentioned in speaking of industrialized care, they have adopted methods and procedures of Fordist industry from the mid-twentieth century: McDonaldization, understood as the industrialization of services, implies the standardization of procedures with the goal of reducing the relational dimension (seen as a hindrance to the search for maximum efficiency). On the user's side, this has implied a deep transformation of the service experience (on which everyone can express their own judgment). At the same time, on the side of those who provide the service, a condition of work has been created that is very similar to an assembly line. Lastly, in the search for economies of scale, these services have tended to be grouped together in large centers, de facto becoming agents of functional and relational desertification of cities (think of the desertifying action of shopping centers, when they push neighborhood shops out of the market and empty out public spaces).

These types of services, and the service society that results, despite still being very widespread, are by now fossils of the past century. In the last twenty years, the picture has become more developed and complex, and an overall view of the service society today shows it as a web of services that are very different by nature, motivations, and social implications.[20] For reasons of simplicity, we can group them into two new types (that go alongside what remains of traditional premodern services, and the many quasi-industrialized services of the last century).

The first type is that of services that live on digital platforms. These services, colonized by neoliberal ideas and practices, have made possible hyper-individualized and disabling service encounters. In the name of ease of use, users have been induced to stay home and be served. And in the name of economic convenience, all relational qualities are eliminated and those who provide the service are forced into a new condition of servitude (a servitude depending on an algorithm). This type of service is obviously what converges in the scenario of the city of everything at/from home and online care, with all of the political and social implications we have already mentioned.

It should be added, though, that this is not the only possible outcome of the use of digital services and platforms. As we will see later (and as Ivana Pais discusses at length in the essay concluding the book), the use of digital platforms and services can lead in the opposite direction. Digital platforms and services can become a digital support for a new type of service, the other new type of service we mentioned at the beginning.[21]

This second new type of service comes from social innovation and is based on the idea that problems are rarely individual, and that they are always better solved collaborating with others.[22] It follows that these services, that we will call *collaborative services*, break with the traditional service model and with the polarities on which it was based, and present an architecture in which the separation between those who provide and those who use, those who are active and passive, those who are experts or not, vanishes.[23] Linked to this first characteristic is another important one for our purposes: they are based on the implicit assumption that each person has skills, and that services have the task of helping that person to implement them. This is, de facto, a practical application of the idea of capability and qualifications proposed some time ago by Amartya Sen and Martha Nussbaum.

Box 3.3 Capabilities and enabling systems

In the 1990s, Amartya Sen and Martha Nussbaum[24] laid the basis for a new approach to the issue of well-being: instead of looking at people as sources of needs to be satisfied, Sen and Nussbaum proposed looking at them as actors having skills that should allow them to act to reach results, such as, for example, "being adequately fed, housed and clothed … being able to move around freely, being able to meet friends and have relationships with them, being able to appear in public without feeling ashamed, being able to communicate and participate, being able to follow one's own creative instincts and so on."[25] By adopting this approach, a person is described as an active subject able to seek well-being by putting their capabilities into practice. Looking at things this way, people are not seen only as sources of needs, but *also* of capabilities; and thus not only as part of the problems that must be faced, but also as actors in their solution. This model of interpretation makes it possible to discuss well-being (both individual and social well-being) shifting attention from the availability of material goods to what they make it possible to achieve; and in particular, to describe what can be achieved in terms of freedom: "freedom from" (hunger, climate adversity, uncertainty, solitude) and "freedom to" (choose where to be and with whom, what work to do and how much, with what ideas and with what image to present oneself to the world). This means that people's well-being is based on their ability to pursue projects, i.e. on their freedom to design how to live, and to live a life that they themselves have, at least in part, autonomously designed. The change in point of view proposed by Sen and Nussbaum has influenced numerous researchers in different disciplines. For designers, it implies a radical change not only in the way of looking at potential users, but also in imagining their own role: from identifying problems and proposing solutions, to identifying not only problems, but above all also latent capabilities and resources, and developing *systems of products and services*, and being able to promote and support them.

To give some simple and well-known examples: collaborative services include *care circles*, in which groups of citizens who share the same problem (for example, they suffer from diabetes, allergies, obesity, or solitude) support and mutually help each other with the supervision of experts (doctors, nurses, or others who are necessary); *collaborative living*, in which the residents of the same building share and manage together the spaces and equipment; *community gardens*, cultivated by neighborhood associations and open to the neighborhoods themselves. Considering these cases, and other similar ones that we could cite, we can observe that, by their collaborative nature, they offer solutions to problems that are otherwise difficult to address. And there is more: they operate as regenerators of the system of proximity in which they are located. In fact, since to function they must be based on collaboration, in reaching concrete results, that are their stated goals, they also produce trust, empathy, and capacity for dialogue, i.e. those social resources that are the weft and warp of every social fabric.

This regenerative capacity is evident in the examples just proposed, for which the collaborative nature is very clear, at all levels: from the quality of the single encounters to the result intended to be reached. But collaborative services are not limited to this. There can be a collaborative approach that extends to and penetrates organizations and sociotechnical systems in which the collaborative character may not be so transparent. Later we will discuss some cases, with reference to the system of care services. Here, we will conclude the digression by stressing the discriminating criterion with which we can define a collaborative approach to services: we can speak of collaborative services when many of the actors involved contribute to reaching a result, providing a contribution in terms of time, energy, attention, knowledge, and ultimately, care. Thus, as we were saying, they go beyond the polarity on which both the traditional services and the hyper-individualized and disabling platforms are based. For this reason, their application is a social innovation for all purposes. Finally, it is again for this same reason that they are a central element in the scenario of the city of proximity and the caring city. In fact, proximity and care can exist only if they are supported by a system of collaborativeervices able to encourage and support them.

3.5 Communities of care

To go from the careless city of distances to the caring city of proximity, it is thus necessary to develop a new generation of collaborative services. This can happen following various paths. The most direct one is to create a service that spurs and supports the construction of communities, and in particular communities of care. To do this, we will return to Hilary Cottam. As a researcher, Cottam has studied many cases, and as a social entrepreneur, she has personally developed some particularly significant ones. The message that emerges is this: whether they are families trapped in the circuit of poverty and marginalization, youth who do not see a future, chronic sick persons, unemployed who no longer believe they can find a job, or elderly persons besieged by solitude, what is necessary first of all is to help them break the isolation and weave a web of relations necessary not only to address single problems, but also to live better the daily life in which they are immersed. In other words, adopting this way of seeing things, we discover that the basis of what people can do or not do in life is the existence – and the quality – of the network of relations they have. Ensuring that these people can construct this network is the type of help they need to emerge from their difficulties. This is a radical form of help[26] because it is based on a different approach to welfare and proposes just as deep a change in the goals to reach, and we add, in the definition of the services to construct.

To make these statements more concrete, let us consider "Circle," a social experiment that Cottam and her team (that at the time was called Participle) imagined, co-designed, and co-produced more than ten years ago. The fact of now having a history, means that it can now be observed and discussed not only as an idea to verify, but as a case of social innovation whose trajectory and results are to be assessed; with the possibility to become a model and point of reference for launching other initiatives.[27]

Circle is an association of elderly people, whose aim is to organize social and cultural initiatives, take care of various practical needs, and by so doing, construct and sustain social connections between the people directly involved, and between them and the support team and the neighborhood. The first prototype was launched in 2007 in collaboration with the Borough of Southwark and the British Ministry of Labour and Social Policy.

The starting point for Circle was a co-design activity that involved over 250 elderly persons and their families. What emerged in the initial listening phase was that the participants mainly wanted three things: *1)* to remain independent and take care of themselves, but having the possibility to be helped by someone for the little things they were no longer able to do alone; *2)* to have a good network of relations, that allowed them a lively social life based on common interests (not only age), and *3)* to share their respective abilities and knowledge, performing some useful activities for the community. Circle was then co-designed to meet these needs of a practical and relational nature, and on express request from the persons involved, was developed so as not to seem like a traditional service, and above all, not to have the participants be seen, and see themselves, as "needy people."

Example 3   *The circle model for the construction of communities*

Circle proposes a service for the elderly based on prevention, support for individual capabilities, and the construction of new communities of care.

This model of services was proposed for the first time by Participle, an English social enterprise, in 2007. Participle constructed a public-private partnership (with the Borough of Southwark and the Ministry of Labour and Social Policy of the United Kingdom) and activated a process of co-design involving over 250 elderly persons and their families. The first prototype was launched in Southwark in 2009. In 2014, not having developed an economically sustainable model yet, the first experiment had to be closed. However, the lessons it left made it possible to go forward with initiatives in the same direction. Today there are various Circles in the United Kingdom, with over 5,000 members and an innovative economic and organizational model that entails collaboration and "horizontal" mutual aid between peers, and "vertical" collaboration with professionals and volunteers. The various activities organized and coordinated by Circle are supported by a dedicated digital platform. Circle's success has been based on the ability of the organizers to start from an existing idea (that of circles of care, which we have already discussed) and use it as the basis to construct a more advanced economic and organizational model. The result emerged from the process of co-design supported by a project-based coalition in which public and private actors, local associations, volunteers, and elderly persons, despite starting from different motivations, succeeded in converging on a common vision and on strategies to implement in order to achieve that vision.

Circle was conceived as a replicable project, with the intention of using this experience to influence welfare culture and policies at the national level. In fact, it was able to show the feasibility of a radically new approach to services for the elderly, based on the construction of communities around the theme of care, and more. This model, in addition to allowing for more efficiently addressing the medical and social problems which traditional welfare has always dealt with, has also reached other goals: it has broken social isolation, helped people live as independently as possible, and not the least, it has reduced the unnecessary use of health services (thus reducing the burden on those services, and the related costs).

What emerged is a detailed *collaborative service* able to promote the skills of each person; guarantee the necessary support when a problem arises; and include various actors with various skills and abilities in the network. In practice, day by day, Circle organized the most varied activities: from an evening playing games at the house of one group member, to mowing the lawn of another; from supporting someone returning home from the hospital, to walking in the park with someone recovering from a stroke; from organizing a field trip, to listening to someone in a moment of difficulty. Then, obviously, there are more serious problems, to be addressed as such. But the continuum of daily activities and difficulties, of moments of mutual assistance and care, constitutes the weft of life. Intervening on it also means preparing for the moments of more acute crisis.

This sum of collaborative micro-services is the most evident aspect of the deeper social process that is the construction of a community. In reality, Circle has been a process of construction of communities; a construction that began with a group of elderly persons and the theme of mutual assisted care, but then went far beyond this to become a community of place, open to various contributions, whose members had abilities and autonomy in organizing the activities that interested them, which also included, when necessary, helping each other or activating the necessary professional support.

This is why it seems we can define it as a "community of care": a community that, due to how it is constructed, is capable of care.

In the case of Circle, all of this took place through the construction of a network of relationships and friendships that the participants autonomously created. Yet it was assisted autonomy: everything they did would not have happened if there had not also been the light, but indispensable support of the Circle team, with its ability to stimulate and sustain initiatives, and when necessary to solve the problems that could inevitably arise from day to day.

What of this experience can be generalized? Certainly, this case tells us a lot about the potential of collaborative services and their architecture. It tells us that there must be a sociotechnical system of proximity in which many service encounters can take place daily (between the elderly, volunteers, and team members). It tells us that in order for this to happen, a set of support services is needed that operates as an enabling system. It also tells us that it is good for this enabling system to include a digital platform with different functions (calendar, coordination, and support for the activities[28]), which allows a small team of professionals to coordinate the activities, respond to specific requests from the members, and cultivate relationships with other social actors in the neighborhood. In other words, the digital platform allows the team to help all of the others be as independent as possible.

Ultimately, what we can take from the case of Circle and extend to the "Circle model," to be replicated in other contexts, are the indications on how to construct communities that are also communities of care; how to rethink welfare based on collaborative services, co-designed and co-produced with the people involved and with the neighborhood; how a dedicated team can stimulate, co-design, and sustain a constellation of initiatives of mutual aid and support, and by so doing, stimulate and mobilize a large quantity of social resources.

This final point is what, ultimately, indicates the direction to take to address the crisis of the system of care services as we have seen it until now: in addition to services whose aim is to provide responses to acute problems (such as those relating to the specialist medical activity of a hospital), it is necessary to providea new and extensive range of enabling services that serve to activate social resources and put people in the condition to help themselves, and each other; and to do so creating capable and informed communities, composed by those who are more directly affected, those who for various reasons can be involved, and those who provide a specific professional contribution.

Adopting this approach thus implies a different representation of the people themselves, whose capabilities (and not only needs) must be considered. But it also implies a new role for the state, a change that is absolutely not the deregulation proposed by McKnight, but a different manner of intervening. In this regard, Cottam writes: "The state is required to play a unique and strong role in the development of a new framework which will set down the guidelines for public investment and ensure all public endeavour is in the service of the new principles. ... the state, currently a mass production organisation will have to undergo its own cultural and organisational revolution."[29]

3.6   Proximity that cares

The Circle model is the expression of a strategy to approach the city that cares. But as mentioned, there can be other paths to this objective. What we will speak of now does not start from the direct construction of communities, but from the action on the system of proximity as a context in which various communities can flourish.

Let us imagine an elderly person who lives alone, or in a couple, in the neighborhood where he has lived for a long time; with the shops and cafés on the corner that he knows (and that know him); with the people he encounters often and greets, and who greet him; with a pharmacy and clinic close to home; with a pleasant community center, a network of professionals who help him in moments of difficulty and who intervene to do what he cannot do by himself, or with his friends and neighbors; and obviously, for possible emergencies. The daily life of this person resembles the way things were in the past (and in part can still be found today in some neighborhoods and villages), but not in the present: today, in general, the situation is very different. Yet, although it is not widespread, this situation is also not an unattainable utopia. It is a project-based vision, something that does not exist but could if the right moves were made, the actions needed to create a new city that cares.

To discuss this, let us again go to Barcelona and take a closer look at the Superilles program we spoke of in Chapter 2. In presenting it and commenting on it we observed that its first phase was the transformation of the use of the streets, going from the monofunction of transport (and parking) to the multifunction of a public space: streets as public spaces open to various possible activities. At the same time, we observed that this initial intervention created the conditions to propose the reorientation on a territorial basis of various public policies: from social services to housing, from taking care of the environment and public green areas, to labor and the regeneration of the democratic life of the city. All of this was observed from the perspective of the evolution of the Superilles program towards a new ecology of the city. Now we can see more closely how things went, and how all of this also leads to the city that cares.

The first phase of the Superilles program, essentially based on the transformation of streets into multifunctional public spaces, was followed by a series of interventions called *Superilles socials*, and a third step is scheduled, called *Superilles integrals*.

Example 4 *Social Superilles and localization of services*

Social Superilles is the name given to a set of innovative practices introduced in Barcelona by the Social Rights Area of the City of Barcelona starting in 2017. It is an initiative based on the experiences of the Superilles program. But while this program was essentially an intervention on the street system with the creation of restricted traffic superblocks (and the transformation of streets into multifunctional public spaces, as we saw in Example 2), Social Superilles intervenes on some social services, first of all those of home care for the elderly.

In fact, the main motivation was the need for a new approach to the problem of the aging of the city's population, an enormous and growing problem. In a city with over 1.6 million inhabitants, people over 65 years old represent 21.3 percent of the population (almost 350,000 people) and those over 75 are 11.2 percent.

It is estimated that by 2030, 8.3 percent of the population will be over 80 years old. Moreover, in Barcelona there are currently more than 90,000 people 65 or older who live alone, that is, 13.6 percent of all family units.30 To address this situation, the central idea was to strengthen home services, reorganizing them on a territorial basis. This entailed two fundamental steps: identify areas in the city which corresponded to a suitable group of residents with the need for this type of service (about 40-60); and organize social workers into teams that are also localized (i.e. linked to a specific area), with the team having the possibility to self-organize work so as to give as much continuity as possible to the relationship with the persons assisted.

To put this idea into practice, the characteristic density of Barcelona certainly helped a great deal: "we can divide the city into hundreds of Social Superilles – writes Lluis Torrens, head of the City's Social Rights Area – ... having a central position (that can be an autonomous logistics base or the emergency room of a hospital or a nursing home) that is 2 or 3 minutes away from each person or family interested in the service. This way, Social Superilles are created that, in the initial phase, involved between 40 and 60 users each, with teams of approximately 12 full-time professionals, who worked planning assistance for the users and making it as personalized and flexible as possible."[31]

Based on the Social Superilles experience, another, more ambitious program was outlined entitled Integral Superilles. The idea is to extend the territorial approach from home services to all of the services relating to the life of citizens.[32] In this case, the reference is to the experience of the micro-areas of Trieste, a strategy for territorial intervention formalized in 2006, but initiated many years earlier with the work of Franco Basaglia and then Francesco Rotelli on mental health.[33]

This complex process of localization is divided into four principal directions: expand the concept of Social Superilles to all activities of care (not only home

services, the starting point); promote and sustain the construction of local communities; operate on public spaces to create a "friendly city" for everyone (and
in particular for children and the elderly); and transform and integrate existing
dwellings to make them suitable for the new demographic structure, and the new
needs of the city. Along with these lines of action, that refer in various ways to
the social dimension of the city, there are two more, of a more general character:
that of the ecology of the city (with the Superilles that also become "ecological
units" on which to construct a sustainable and resilient city), and that of democracy (with the Superilles and the communities that live in them as agents of a
renewed participatory democracy).

The core of the Social Superilles is the territorialization of home care
services, through a reorganization of the operators and their work at the
neighborhood level, that creates a social service of proximity. Speaking of
how he sees the future of services for the elderly, Lluis Torrens has written: "The underlying idea is what we call the distributed virtual residence:
a situation in which a person in their own home receives the same services
they would receive in the room of a neighborhood nursing home."[34] Moving in this direction requires creating a new system of services: in order for
each elderly person to be assisted and supported as if they were indeed in a
nursing home, it is necessary to reorganize the system adopting a distributed architecture, indicating small, well-defined areas which correspond
to a just as well-defined group of residents (with care needs) and social
operators dedicated to them. It is also necessary for these operators to be
able to get organized rapidly and flexibly, to follow the daily evolution of
needs. Lastly, at the center of this area there must be an operational base
which the operators can rely on for their daily activities.

It is clear that, if this is the situation, home care services become more
effective and improve working conditions (because the operators don't
have the stress and waste of time of having to move around different
parts of the cities). Similarly, there are also advantages in terms of quality
of the service offered because for the operators there are more possibilities
and more time to relate to the persons assisted. That is not all: by forming
stable teams dedicated to the neighborhood in which they operate, which
have their logistical base in the neighborhood itself, the service and the
operators that make it up are an entity that is more recognizable by local
residents and organizations.[35] This allows them to become something
more than a provider of specific home services for those who need them;

it allows them to enter into contact with the other residents as well, and to create a network of relationships between these persons and the more fragile or marginalized members of the area, thus contributing to the construction of a new local community; a community that is born around the theme of care, and for which this service is one of the promoters.

However, a community like this one, that aspires to be a community of care, is not made up of only social services, however distributed and close to the people they may be. Here we come to the third phase of the program, defined as the Integral Superilles. For this part of the program, the goal is to extend the territorialization of the services to the entire urban infrastructure, i.e. to rethink the entire system of proximity, from social housing to green areas, to the supply of energy, as services of proximity. By setting this goal, the Integral Superilles program tends to offer citizens the possibility to find everything they need in their daily life close to home (in the case of Barcelona, less than ten minutes from where they are located).

More precisely, Integral Superilles aim to coordinate the health service with services relating to social housing, and with the activities of neighborhood associations and the social enterprises that operate there; and in doing this, not only coordinate and improve the services that are already offered, but also make other initiatives possible, giving life to new places for encounters, coworking spaces, or shared services for collaborative living.[36] Lluis Torrens writes: "to precisely coordinate the programs and services of social assistance, it is necessary to take into account the territorial scale. Spatial proximity is essential in economic and ecological terms, from the perspective of truly democratic governance, and that of the management and quality of services for communities."[37]

In the background of this program, as for that proposed by Hilary Cottam, there is the idea of starting from personal capabilities and thus from considering people not only as bearers of problems, but also as part of their solution (as we have seen in Box 3.3). This common approach, though, leads to the emergence of a different strategy, that is complementary to that proposed by Cottam. The Circle model, in fact, starts by constructing a community capable of care, knowing that in order to exist, it will also require a system of proximity that supports it.[38] In the case of the Barcelona Superilles, on the other hand, the process is practically symmetrical: the existing system of proximity is integrated with new services to make it possible and probable for everyone (including the most fragile subjects) to recreate their web of relations; and thus to participate in the construction of new communities.

The importance of this way of doing things could have already been recognized and stressed years ago (indeed, this is what happened). Now, the tragedy of Covid-19 confirms it: we have all been able to see the need to have an ecosystem of care that is well-rooted and widespread in the local territory; that is, to have a proximity that cares.[39]

3.7   Care, communities, and hybrid proximities

What we have said to this point refers to ways of considering the relationship between proximity, community, and care from the perspective of creating a city that cares, today. When discussing the examples, we mentioned the fact that what happened was sustained by services and digital platforms, and all of this was proposed as a condition of normality, as if to say that everyone uses electricity and the road network. However, although the use of digital services and platforms has become normal, its novelty, and the dimension of the transformation that it has brought (and that it will likely bring in the future) are such as to make it useful to concentrate on its current and possible implications, for various reasons.

The first is to make it clear that here we are considering a use of digital technologies aimed at supporting and promoting care activities whose center is found in the interactions that take place in the physical world. We know, however, that a powerful trend is underway that goes in exactly the opposite direction: that in which teleassistance and domestic robotics are understood as substituting medical and social activities to be carried out in physical presence, denying the profound nature of the relationship of care, and as already said, transforming assistance into a form of teleabandonment (and becoming central components of the dystopian scenario of everything at/from home).

In the cases we have considered here, though, this is not the case: digital services and platforms are used as tools to support and facilitate physical encounters, as experiments of what could and should be done to live better in the hybrid physical and digital space that we all inhabit now. In fact, if we define as hybrid something that has a physical and a digital dimension at the same time, it can be stated that the care, community, and proximity we have spoken of to this point, are hybrid: despite being rooted in the physical world, they could not exist without a digital component (composed of infrastructure, platforms, special services, and applications). It should be added that the importance of this hybrid dimension has become very evident with the pandemic, the limits on mobility it has entailed, and the physical distancing it has required.

At the beginning of the chapter (and in Box 3.1 in particular), we already observed how and how much the shifting of the center of gravity of daily life towards the digital world influences scenarios of proximity, and thus of care. Certainly, the more linear of the potential outcomes is that all of this will strengthen the scenario of everything at/from home and online care, in the version of teleabandonment. But we have also seen that there are examples in which the obligation of distancing has led to inventing modes of care without direct contact, while still maintaining a relational and functional proximity;[40] being close, that is, even without being able to touch each other. What makes this possible is the opportunity that the digital world gives us to be in contact not only with those who are very far away physically, but also with those who are in proximity, those with whom I can not only exchange music and photographs, but also practical favors, such as going shopping or getting something from the pharmacy. This indicates an interesting strategy for the use, and consequently the development, of the digital world: that of also, and above all, cultivating relations between "neighbors," i.e. between well-defined interlocutors located in a physical space of proximity. Taking this direction means developing a new generation of platforms conceived precisely for this purpose: tools to stimulate and support encounters in the digital space that lead to encounters in physical space; in other words, tools for a new hybrid proximity.[41]

Discussing the new hybrid nature of the spaces, and of proximity, another observation is necessary, though. To this point, hybrid has meant physical-digital. But the term can also have another meaning, that of a space in which different activities are combined (and that, traditionally, took place in dedicated places). For example, newsstands that are also town service counters; laundromats in which people can work (for online jobs); and cafés which become concierges. These are the cases most frequently referred to when speaking of hybrid places. But after all, streets are hybrid as well, such as in Barcelona, where it is said that they are not infrastructures dedicated to traffic, but public spaces open to many different uses (including mobility). Ultimately, the diversified proximity to which we aspire is also hybrid, since it can be seen as the hybridization of different functional proximities.

These two forms of hybridization, physical-digital and functional, have different stories and motivations (and can occur independent of each other). Yet there is also a strong correlation between them. In particular, today the spread of the second meaning, that of functional hybrids, is strongly linked to that of the first, of physical-digital hybrids. In fact, the digital dimension of the systems that they are generating allows for creating networks of distributed services in whose nodes various activities can coexist, relating to different service systems. For example, still remaining in Barcelona, the Radars project contributes to producing hybrid spaces in both of the senses just mentioned. For the social services the question was: how to identify at a detailed level cases of solitude, sickness, and marginalization that are not easily visible? The response found was the creation of a network of people with strong roots in the neighborhood, who function as antennas in the local territory. In practice, since many residents of the neighborhood continuously frequent certain places (like newsstands, cafés, and pharmacies) and establish relations of familiarity with those who manage them, such people can notice if something is wrong, if certain people don't appear any more or if someone has problems. When this happens, these people connect with the social services to report the case. As we see, the system is very simple, and with its digital component it is even simpler. Nevertheless, it could not work if there were no longer shops and public spaces of proximity in the neighborhood; but also if the Radars platform were not present, that allows everyone to interact easily.

Example 5   *Radars: a network of human sensors*

Radars is a program sponsored by the City of Barcelona to identify people at risk of isolation and exclusion. Started in 2008, it was conceived for people over 75, who live alone or with another elderly person (over 65), and also for those who, despite having limited autonomy, live alone and without a network of support.[42] In practice, a "radar" network is created that can include neighbors, but also the shopkeepers and neighborhood associations, and so on. They agree to keep contact with the elderly persons in their area and to inform the social services operators if they detect any criticalities. The network also involves medical cen-

ters and neighborhood pharmacies, that are called on to intervene when necessary as "specialized radars."
Radars also promotes initiatives in connection with neighborhood organizations
(volunteer associations, but also civic centers, libraries, etc.) to favor the connection between the elderly and their neighbors with the goal of combatting isolation
and creating new forms of communities.

Another example in this same direction brings us to Milan, where the City has instituted WeMi, the Welfare Milan program. In this case, the digital dimension is given by a series of services offered on a platform. Their characteristic is that they have specific roots in the physical world. This is because from the start, the choice was to create, at the same time, the digital platform and a network of spaces, called WeMi Spaces, located in cafés or other places already frequented by neighborhood residents.

As regards the platform, its stated purpose is to operate at three levels: as a "sensor," a "broker," and a "facilitator."[43] Being an open system in which in principle everyone can present their needs and pose their questions, the platform can operate as a sensor able to recognize the needs that services organized in a traditional form could not bring out. On the other hand, it can operate as a terrain in which, clearly and transparently, the supply and demand for social services can meet (presented in a sort of large catalogue of proposals certified and guaranteed by the city administration). Lastly, the integration between the platform and the WeMi Spaces, that are distributed around the city and integrated with other activities, favors the creation of a fabric of local relations, laying the basis for new forms of communities in which citizens, the public entity, and social workers can together pose problems and seek answers in a collaborative form.

Example 6 *WeMi: a platform and many hybrid places*

The WeMi project was activated by the City of Milan in 2015. Its architecture is based on two pillars: a digital platform (the WeMi Platform) and a network of physical spaces (the WeMi Spaces).
The WeMi platform proposes five categories of services (offered by the City and by partner entities): personal well-being, support for families, management of domestic activities, socialization and sharing, and financial education. There are many types of services offered: from the home delivery of meals to nursing

> assistance, from transport with specially equipped vehicles to various services supporting families, such as: the search for caregivers, domestic help, babysitters, support for studying, support for disabilities, family mediation, pet care, support for home maintenance, the performance of small errands, and the purchase and home delivery of medicines. In addition to this catalogue of services, the platform is also a digital place in which citizens can freely exchange experiences and organize new initiatives.
>
> The WeMi Spaces (there are currently 16) are the physical interface of the platform. They are managed by associations and cooperatives in concert with the City of Milan, and are situated in existing places, that have their own life and motivations, independent of those of WeMi but compatible with them (such as cafés, community centers, cultural centers, etc.). Over time, the WeMi Spaces have become consolidated and established roots, also becoming centers for encounters, discussion, and mutual support among citizens.

This last point is very important because it has meant that the WeMi Spaces have become centers for encounters and initiatives in neighborhoods. In them, the citizens find what the spaces were originally conceived for (personnel who advise them on how to find the welfare services most suited to their respective needs). But they find other things as well, because these people help them weave a web of relations, to enter into contact with each other and plan initiatives to develop together.

What characterizes this program is thus its strongly hybrid character, not only because it combines digital interactions with "in person" interactions; and not only because it was established in existing places, making them functionally hybrid, but also because it makes the roles hybrid, mixing the activities of professional care with those of volunteer work and those among neighbors, friends, and acquaintances.

To summarize, these hybrid spaces become generative because they allow for reaching different and unexpected results. As we have seen, they help citizens orient themselves in the offer of services (that otherwise would be difficult to reach), allowing those who provide services to observe new demands and orient their proposals accordingly (so as to tailor supply to actual demand), and by aggregating citizens and other social actors at the local level around common interests and collaborative activities, they become enabling systems for the construction of communities, communities that are hybrid, but at the same time strongly rooted in the neighborhood.

3.8   Redistributing care work

The examples cited to this point confirm the relationship between care and proximity, and indicate ways to approach the city that cares. Now, considering them together, we can draw some indications of a general nature. The first concerns care understood as time, attention, energy, and required skills; in brief, care as work to be performed (again, see Box 3.2). Observed from this standpoint, all of the projects proposed until now are *also* ways to distribute care work among multiple persons, and first of all among those directly involved.

The initial assumption is that everyone has the desire to be autonomous (and thus to take care of themselves), and that many would be willing to take care of others, i.e. of someone with difficulties, if they had the possibility to do so. This second desire, however, clashes with a reality in which it is difficult to do so alone: taking care of someone or something requires an assumption of responsibility, attention, skills, and time to invest, that are – or appear – too much to be placed on a single individual's shoulders. Dealing with this reality, the idea common to all of the cases proposed thus corresponds to a dual response: reduce overall care work by making people who potentially need care as autonomous as possible, and distribute the remaining care work among multiple people, such that by acting together and collaboratively, each person can take a part of the work, based on their own possibilities (i.e. their skills and available time).

The elderly of Circle, for example, are put in a condition to mutually care for each other, and the care work that remains is divided among volunteers and professionals. This action of reducing and distributing the workload by caring for each other is the heart of all collaborative services. This can happen with an *exchange among peers*, as in Circle and in all other care circles; or it can be a symbiotic exchange between different but complementary elements, such as *intergenerational exchange*, when an association makes possible the encounter of youth and the elderly, for example, by organizing forms of collaborative life;[44] or also, when there is a need to care for someone with serious problems, it can be the creation around this person of a *care network*, that distributes the responsibilities and workload among family members, friends, and neighbors, coordinated by a dedicated platform.[45] An analogous logic is found in the case of the Social Superilles of Barcelona, where a system of proximity is achieved in which elderly people can live autonomously with the support of some professionals, but also relying on what is offered in the neighborhood, meaning the widespread assumption of responsibility by neighbors, shopkeepers, and local associations.

To generalize, social innovation tells us that it is possible to make good use of the capacity for care that each person has. To do so, it is necessary for appropriate services to be available that allow for catalyzing and coordinating various and fragmented contributions of care, giving them continuity and consistency.

Starting from this lesson, we can see the city that cares as an ecosystem of various communities in which care work is distributed, involving a great number of people, groups, and institutions, with different skills and responsibilities (from those of highly-specialized professionals, to those of family members, friends, and neighbors with no specific knowledge, limited availability of time, but a lot of good will). Given the intrinsic relationship between care and physical contact, these caring communities are also communities of place, communities whose members are close and operate in the same system of proximity.

This description of the caring city as a set of capable communities (i.e. capable of care) could also be given in the past; but then, the communities were the result of the slow coevolution of urban and social forms. Today, in order for these communities to exist, and to carry out this redistribution of care work, choices must be made, some rules defined, and a system of enabling platforms and collaborative services created.

In order for all of this to happen, and to expand beyond the cases of social innovation such as those which we have examined here, a way needs to be found to activate a virtuous circle between social, technical, and institutional innovation that leads to the generation of a great number of these caring communities. Yet that is not enough; a profound cultural change is needed. At its center is a different conception of time: the distribution of care work among many people may never become the new normal if at the same time we don't give new value to care time, which is actually the value of time *tout court*.

Social innovation can tell us something in this area as well.

3.9   A new ecology of time

The second indication of a general nature that we can draw from the cases we have discussed concerns time, and the recognition of its different qualities.

The localization of social services in the home in Barcelona and in other cities where this has been done, reduces forced travel time for care workers; simultaneously, the relational nature of the service proposed requires more time for each single encounter. Similarly, the existence of a digital platform, by reducing the time necessary to carry out administrative activities, allows the Circle team to interact with a large number of members of the association. On the other hand, the very idea of Circle implies dedicating more time to each encounter and each initiative promoted.

To generalize: the city of proximity has a contradictory relationship with time. On the one hand, it means saving time, while on the other hand, it requires time. The functional proximity it proposes gives time (that saved in undesired travel), while relational proximity requires time (that necessary to establish and maintain relationships of care). The balance between the two, though, cannot be assessed in a banal manner, as if the time we are speaking of were always the same: the undesired travel time saved is time without quality, the contrary of that required to provide care. Therefore, since these two types of time are not comparable, we cannot say whether in general terms the city of proximity and care requires more or less time that the city of distances, without care. What we can say with certainty, is that it requires developing a new vision of time: the single, accelerated time of modernity must be transformed into the *plural time* of the caring city; a plural time, because it does not exclude fast time, but recognizes and appreciates also, and perhaps above all, slow time.

In this framework, the appreciation of slow time has a practical reason: care, and thus also the quality of everything that is done with care, requires time, both on the part of those who produce this quality of things done with care, and those who simply appreciate it. In fact, for any entity to which we refer (a product, an event, or in our case, an interaction), the quality of "done with care" is what results from a process that is able to address the intrinsic complexity and uniqueness of what is done and the context in which it is placed; and this necessarily requires time. In the case of care work, the interactions that are produced and the context in which they take place are necessarily complex and unique.

Thus, a work of care, that is truly such, requires time, and the time of care is slow time.

Giving value to slowness, and to the quality of "done with care," therefore does not depend on a purely aesthetic choice (we seek slowness because we like slow things – as in a sort of reverse futurism). Rather, it is the result of recognizing that we want to slow down because we seek quality that can be created and appreciated only if we take the time to do so;[46] that is, if we slow down. Hilary Cottom stresses often in her writings how much time she spent with the people with whom she intended to develop new ideas of service. We hear the same thing from whomever is involved in activities of care and does them not as a duty, but because they want to do them: to do things well takes time. All of this leads us also to say that care has an intrinsically artisanal nature, in the meaning Richard Sennet attributes to this term in his book *The Craftsman*,[47] when he writes that an artisan is someone who does something with the principal aim of doing it well, up to standard. Therefore – we add – doing it with care, dedicating the time necessary.

All of this leads to a central question for our discussion: care does not require only tactility and thus proximity, as de la Bellacasa has taught us to recognize. By its very nature, it requires time. Therefore, care can never be "machine-made," according to a Fordist, automated model, using digital technologies and artificial intelligence. The center of activity of care, the encounter in which the exchange takes place, must be "handmade," with the necessary attention and time. This does not mean rejecting technology (the craftsman Sennett speaks of does not reject it and does not aspire to return to models from the past). But the technological apparatus we have today must be conceived as a support system so that things can be done with quality, and thus with care. In our case, this means giving people the time necessary to become closer to each other, and to everything that surrounds them.

3.10   Density and economies of proximity

The question of care work and the time necessary to perform it, becoming intertwined, brings us to the economy of the city that cares. The theme is enormous, and we will limit ourselves to just a few notes that in this case as well, are drawn from experiences of social innovation and the examples proposed. The key words are density, diversity, and economy of proximity.

The city of proximity must be a dense city. We have already discussed this in Chapter 2, and we defined it as horizontal density, consisting of streets, squares, cafés, shops, and public parks where it is possible for people to encounter each other and where it is likely that these encounters will evolve into conversations, and thus into collaborative projects and activities of care. The cases considered beforehand show this: Circle would have met with difficulties in implementation if there had not been a sufficient number of people interested in proximity: volunteers, professionals, and commercial activities willing to join the project. For its part, WeMi was able to avoid being a simple digital platform because it found a fertile ground of public places of proximity in which to locate its spaces. Lastly, in the case of Barcelona, the territorialization of social services carried out with the Social Superilles was successful because it drew on and enhanced the existing urban density. In fact, the home care personnel was able to organize their activities at the local level as a service in proximity because the urban density meant that in a relatively limited area there was the necessary user basin to justify the service.

This close observation therefore gives us a generalizable indication concerning the economy of services we have spoken of:[48] the territorial organization of care activities, and of the collaborative services on which they are based, is more effective if we refer to a sufficiently dense system of proximity. Thus, promoting sufficiently dense systems of proximity is a necessary step to move towards the city that cares.

This first, elementary observation can be followed by a second, that is more complex: a service that supports an activity of care is more likely to exist and last if it operates in a system of diversified proximity. Only thus can an *economy of proximity* be achieved, i.e. an economy based on various activities, operating close to each other, and mutually supporting each other. The theme of the economy of proximity still needs to be developed. The examples provided, and social innovation in general, though, indicate certain paths for experimentation.

One of these is given by the functional hybridizations that often characterize the new proposals, which we have already mentioned: the city services located in a café not only have the relational motivational to make them closer to people's daily life, but also to create an economy of scope based on the symbiosis of the two activities that join together and support each other; a symbiosis that in order to function requires proximity. This specific example tells us something that could have a more general value: functional hybridization, combined with that of roles and sustained by digital hybridization, could be the path to follow to achieve a new economy of proximity. What is certain is that to imagine this new economy, it is necessary to think of it in its potential context. The economy of proximity not only must not seek its functioning in the past, but must also not be imagined as a linear evolution of what it has been until now. It must be able to locate itself in the world that is emerging, a world where the various crises we are experiencing change the perception of priorities (for example, the urgency of an ecological transition) and roles (for example, the new role of the state); and where technology is revolutionizing the way things can be done. Ivana Pais, in the essay that concludes this book, tells us that a new generation of digital platforms could emerge, conceived as "local collective goods for collaboration"; perhaps this is exactly what it would be useful to create.

Lastly, and this is the most delicate aspect, it is necessary to discuss how to recognize a value produced when it does not have – and perhaps cannot and should not have – a monetary equivalent. For example, today it has become entirely evident that a neighborhood shop also plays a fundamental social role, as a component of the city that cares. This social role should thus be added to the reasons that justify its existence. But: how can we evaluate this contribution? How can we provide compensation for it?

Analogously, we have said and repeated that the caring city does not require only care professionals but also a widespread attitude of care on everyone's part: how can we evaluate it and provide compensation for it, assuming that, in this case, for many it would not be financial compensation? More in general: how much is work worth – care work, in our case – when it is done the way it should be (with care, that is)?

Returning to the idea of artisanal work proposed by Richard Sennet,[49] we could say that the value of care work done with care is found, or should be found, principally in the satisfaction of those who know they have done things well, i.e. with care. But although this can be a good starting point, it is not yet a satisfactory response to our questions.

Notes

[1] This beautiful expression was used by Franco Rotelli, director of the Department of Mental Health of Trieste, in reference to the issue of the mental health in the city and the revolutionary way of addressing it begun by Franco Basaglia in the 1970s. See: Franco Basaglia, *L'utopia della realtà*, Turin, Einaudi, 2005; Franco Rotelli, "Servizi che intrecciano storie," in *L'arte della cura nella medicina di comunità a Trieste: storie e racconti di malattia*, edited by Giovanna Gallio, Trieste, ENAIP, 2013.

[2] Berenice Fisher, Joan C. Tronto, "Toward a Feminist Theory of Caring," in E. Abel, M. Nelson (eds.), *Circles of Care*, Albany, SUNY Press, 1990, p. 37; Joan C. Tronto, *Moral Boundaries. A Political Argument for an Ethic of Care*, New York, Routledge, 1993 (Italian trans. *Confini morali. Un argomento politico per l'etica della cura*, Reggio Emilia, Diabasis, 2006).

[3] de la Bellacasa, *Matters of Care*, cit.

[4] Maria Puig de la Bellacasa also suggests modifying the definition of care developed by Joan Tronto and Berenice Fischer, extending it to the interaction between everything that is a part of the web of life. "Care," de la Bellacasa writes, modifying the definition given by Jane Tronto, "is everything that is done (rather than everything that 'we' do) to maintain, continue, and repair 'the world' so that all (rather than 'we') can live in it as well as possible" (de la Bellacasa, *Matters of care*, cit., p. 161). By doing this, de la Bellacasa brings the idea of care outside of its traditional anthropocentrism, considering it a relational modality that goes beyond the human. When we take care of what surrounds us, recognizing our interdependence, we actually begin to join the deeper structure of the terrestrial ecosystem, its relational ontology. Manzini, Tassinari, "Designing Down to Earth," cit.

[5] de la Bellacasa, *Matters of Care*, cit.

[6] Júlia Benini, Ezio Manzini, Lekshmy Parameswaran, "Care Up, Close and Digital. A Designers' Outloook on the Pandemic in Barcelona," *Design and Culture*, 13(1), 2021, pp. 91-102. DOI: 10.1080/17547075.2021.1880694.

[7] Ibid.

[8] "Cura," *Treccani Vocabolario on line*, www.treccani.it.

[9] The theme of care, linked to that of care work and gender inequality has a vast literature, that obviously includes the authors already cited, Berenice Fisher, Joan Tronto, and Maria Puig de la Bellacasa. Recently, a book was published in Italy as well that presents the reflections and indications on this theme of an English working group called The Care Collective: The Care Collective, *Manifesto per la cura. Per una politica dell'interdipendenza*, Rome, Alegre, 2021 (original edition: *The Care Manifesto. The Politics of Interdependence*, London, Verso, 2020).

[10] This motivation is also linked to other reasons of different types, of which we will cite only one very objective one here: the number of children is decreasing, along with the possibility for them to form groups in the immediate vicinity of their homes, leading the need for parents to take their children to places dedicated to various activities of socialization.

[11] John McKnight, *The Careless Society. Community and Its Counterfeits*, New York, Basic Books, 1995.

[12] Hilary Cottam, *Radical Help. How We Can Remake the Relationships Between Us and Revolutionise the Welfare State*, London, Virago, 2018.

[13] Given these problems, the solution that is proposed is based on the application of criteria of efficiency (what is called "New Public Management"). According to Cottam, instead of resolving the problem, this perspective makes it worse, maintaining the underlying idea that for every problem there must be a service; the entire question is reduced to this: how to produce services in the cheapest way possible. But even accepting this idea of cost savings as a solution, there are no economies to be achieved that allow for such a broad and continuative increase of the number of people needing a service.

[14] It should be noted that this impossibility would also take place in the neoliberal society of privatized services, and in the welfare society, as we have known it until now in Europe. This is because, ultimately, both of the models have adopted the same idea of service.

[15] The Care Lab, "Today's Care Emergency reveals tomorrow's System of Care," https://medium.com/, April 7, 2020.

[16] For an introduction to services and their design, see Lara Penin, *An Introduction to Service Design. Designing the Invisible*, London-New York-Oxford-Delhi-Sydney, Bloomsbury, 2018; Anna Meroni, Daniela Sangiorgi, *Design for Services*, London, Grower, 2011.

[17] "(fig.) Object, event, or situation that forces a certain behavior or that strongly limits freedom of action" ("servitù" in the *Treccani Vocabolario on line*, www.treccani.it).

[18] The distinction between service and servitude has been posed very clearly by Giorgio De Michelis, "La Pubblica Amministrazione dalla servitù al servizio," *Queste Istituzioni*, 99, 1994.

[19] See the critique of McKnight, but also, and above all, that of Ivan Illic. McKnight, *The Careless Society*, cit.; Ivan Illich, *Deschooling society*, New York, Harper & Row, 1971 (Italian trans. *Descolarizzare la società*, Mondadori, Milano, 1983); Ivan Illich, *Tools for Conviviality*, London, Calder and Boyars, 1973 (Italian trans. *La convivialità*, Como, Red Edizioni, 1993).

[20] Manzini, *Design When Everybody Designs*, cit.

[21] Ezio Manzini, Massimo Menichinelli, "Platforms for Re-localization. Communities and Places in the Postpandemic Hybrid Spaces," *Strategic Design Research Journal*, 14(1), January-April 2021.

[22] Richard Sennett, *Together. The Rituals, Pleasures, and Politics of Cooperation*, New Haven, Yale University Press, 2012 (Italian trans. *Insieme. Rituali, piaceri, politiche della collaborazione*, Milan, Feltrinelli, 2014).

[23] François Jegou, Ezio Manzini, *Collaborative Services. Social Innovation and Design for Sustainability*, Polidesign, Milan, 2008. For an in-depth discussion of the relational dimension of collaborative services: Carla Cipolla, "Solutions for Relational Services," in S. Miettnen, A. Valtonen, (eds.), *Service Design with Theory. Discussions on Change, Value and Methods*, Lapland, Lapland University Press (LUP), 2011. DOI: 10.13140/RG.2.1.3013.7201; Ead., "Designing for Vulnerability: Interpersonal Relations and Design, She Ji," *The Journal of Design, Economics, and Innovation*, 4(1), 2018, pp. 111-122, DOI: https://doi.org/10.1016/j.sheji.2018.03.001; Carla Cipolla, Ezio Manzini, "Relational Services," *Knowledge, Technology and Policy*, 22, 2009.

[24] Amartya Sen, Martha Nussbaum (eds.), *The Quality of Life*, New York, Oxford University Press, 1993.

[25] Ibid. (from the Introduction).

[26] Cottam, *Radical Help*, cit.

[27] Hilary Cottam, Cath Dillon, *The Learning from London Circle*, July 2014, pdf available at http://www.participle.net/.

[28] Operating using the platform as a tool to coordinate all of the activities also has the important implication that, thanks to the platform, it is possible to record everything done in a non-invasive manner, thus gathering the information that is needed to then assess the results reached.

[29] Hilary Cottam, *Revolution 5.0. A Social Manifesto*, December 10, 2019, pdf available at https://www.hilarycottam.com/

[30] BCNEcologia – Barcelona Urban Ecology Agency, *Planificació d'una nova divisió territorial del Servei d'Assistència Domiciliària (SAD)*, report not published, Àrea de Drets Socials, Ajuntament de Barcelona, 2019.

[31] Lluis Torrens, *Ageing and Improving Public Management. The Case of Barcelona and the Social Superblocks*, Transjus, Institut de Recerca, Facultat de Dret, Univesitat de Barcelona, 2018, pdf available at http://diposit.ub.edu/dspace/

[32] Lluis Torrens, Sebastià Riutort, Marta Juan, "Towards a New Social Model of the City: Barcelona's Integral Superblocks," in Oliver Heckmann (ed.), *Future Urban Habitation*, New York, John Wiley & Sons, in the course of publication.

[33] Rotelli, "Servizi che intrecciano storie," cit.; Francesco Salvini, *Le ecologie che curano*, April 2019, pdf available at https://transversal.at/

[34] Torrens, *Ageing and Improving Public Management*, cit.

[35] These local bases are important from various standpoints, and are spreading. An example is the Enabling Village in Singapore, described as a "integrated inclusive community space, home to several social businesses and community services, with a special focus on training and employment of people with disabilities – where caregivers can organize peer support sessions, receive ongoing support and training programs as well as enjoy some rest and respite." (see https://enablingvillage.sg/, cited in Parameswaran Herczeg, Dordas Perpinyà, Garcia i Mateu, "Social Design: Principles & Practices to Foster Caring Urban Communities," in Heckmann (ed.), *Future Urban Habitation*, cit.)

[36] Torrens, Retort, Juan, "Towards a New Social Model of the City," cit.

[37] Torrens, *Ageing and Improving Public Management*, cit.

[38] If that system is not present, or is not sufficient, it is the same community in construction that must succeed in adapting what exists, activating the spaces and functions that are necessary for it.

[39] A way of being in the local territory that does not mean only to control it, but also the capacity to make it become a platform for action. In the case of Covid-19, this means the widespread capacity to do tests and vaccinations, to isolate some areas when necessary and in a differentiated manner, and to invite and help people to behave as requested. The Care Lab, "Today's Care Emergency reveals tomorrow's System of Care," cit.

[40] Benini, Manzini, Parameswaran, "Care Up, Close and Digital," cit.

[41] Manzini, Menichinelli, "Platforms for Re-localization," cit.

[42] See the page "Projecte Radars" on the site of the City of Barcelona https://www.barcelona.cat/ca/

[43] See https://wemi.comune.milano.it; Fondazione Cariplo, "A Milano il welfare è di tutti," http://welfareinazione.fondazionecariplo.it/it/, January 2, 2020.

[44] An example of this type is *Prendi a casa uno studente*, a Milano (see https://www.meglio.milano.it/prendi-in-casa/).

[45] An example of this type is *Tyze* in Canada (see http://tyze.com).

[46] The ideas proposed here are an extrapolation of those proposed, from the beginning, by Slow Food (see Carlo Petrini, *Buono, pulito e giusto. Principi di nuova gastronomia*, Turin, Einaudi, 2005). In particular, the reflection on the relationship between time and quality was inspired by a conference held many years ago by Cinzia Scaffidi at the International Slow + Design Seminar, Milan, October 6, 2006.

[47] Richard Sennett, *The Craftsman*, New Haven, Yale University Press, 2008 (Italian trans. *L'uomo artigiano*, Milan, Feltrinelli, 2008).

[48] This economic criterion is valid for any type of service, also for more collaborative services, and ones that are further away from a market economy. In fact, each service, and each service encounter, has its own economy: it can be done and can last in time if the relationship between what is obtained and what must be spent is manageable. This is also true in an economy that is not only monetary, in which what is spent is time, attention, and energy brought to bear in a non-commercial manner.

[49] Sennett, *The Craftsman*, cit.

4　Designing to Bring Close

The music starts. A man gets up from the table, crosses the floor, and asks a lady at another table if she wants to dance. She agrees. Although they don't know each other, both know what to do and begin to dance. They say a few words, perhaps beginning a conversation; perhaps the conversation continues after the dance.

This scene can seem like a nostalgic way of being, doing, and dancing from the past. Yet it tells us a lot about how people can be helped to approach each other, how encounters can be facilitated, and what can be designed to make that happen.

The scene as proposed above is certainly not the result of a conscious, unitary design. Rather, it is the result of a coevolution of the various elements that make up that system of proximity: the dance hall, the music, the ability to dance, and two people willing to meet each other. All of this, obviously, does not predetermine what will actually happen. It does not tell us if the conversation between the two will be pleasant, if and how it will continue after that first encounter. The dance floor, music, and shared knowledge of the rules of dancing are only what makes an encounter more likely.

The example of the dance floor and the dancers also tells us what the contemporary city no longer is, but could be. The current city, the city of distances, is by its nature hostile to encounters and their possibility to evolve into conversations, shared projects, and communities. In the previous chapters we have seen the need, and the possibility, to change orientation and move in an opposite direction, towards a city of proximity, which is also a city that cares.

In this chapter we will see what can be done for this change to occur; that is, in practice, how and what to design to create closeness. So, returning to the initial image: what can be done for there to be welcoming dance floors, stimulating music, and a widespread ability to dance? What can be done today to create systems of proximity in which people come closer and encounter each other? And what can be done so that these encounters evolve into conversations and new communities?

The short answer is: encounters, conversations, and communities, because of their relational nature, cannot be designed directly. They can, however, be made possible and probable, by making the ecosystem in which they operate more favorable. To do this, it is necessary to design the material and digital artifacts that make them practically possible, that we will call *technical and social infrastructure* (the characteristics of the dance hall and the fact that people know how to dance), and those that induce and orient the encounters, that we will call *stimulants* and *attractors* (the music in the dance hall).

4.1   Technical and social infrastructure as platforms of opportunity

The city of proximity that we would like to contribute to creating is a project-based scenario and not a utopian proposal. This is because – as must be the case for all design-orienting scenarios[1] – it is not only a vision but also a set of guidelines on what needs to be done to put it into practice; that is, in concrete terms, how to start from the point where we are (the city of distances) and take steps towards where we would like to go (the city of proximity). The basis of what can make this step possible is the design of infrastructure consistent with the idea of livable proximity and the process that leads to creating it.

The most common meaning of "infrastructure" refers to sociotechnical systems able to sustain various productive and reproductive activities (supplying them with energy, water, mobility, and digital networks). This technical infrastructure must then be accompanied by social infrastructure,[2] that allows for providing different types of services of a social nature (schools, universities, hospitals, health care facilities, public housing, courts, and prisons). Often, in addition to infrastructure as such, this term refers to the process that leads to constructing it (for this meaning, the term *infrastructuring* is used[3]).

Traditionally, the infrastructure we speak of is the result of large, centralized projects, but a more careful look leads us to recognizing something else: the existence of micro-infrastructuring and self-produced infrastructuring processes. In Chapter 2, we mentioned how, after a catastrophe, places and products can be used for purposes other than those that were foreseen in normal conditions,[4] and how this phenomenon takes place also in normal conditions when certain artifacts conceived for a specific purpose (public spaces or digital platforms), over time are able to support other, new and unforeseen activities.[5] Here we can add that, considering social innovation and its evolutionary trajectories, we observe that, before reaching maturity, and the construction of dedicated infrastructure, there is a phase of *self-infrastructuring*, in which groups of creative and enterprising people (social inventors) modify the sense and use of what they find, to transform it into the infrastructure necessary for what they seek to do. Thus an abandoned plot of land can become a garden, a busy street a bike path, a parking lot a space for tables, a residential building a cohousing project, and so on. And this takes place before the decisions necessary to transform the self-generated infrastructure into fully legitimate and consolidated infrastructure are made.

The result is that the process of infrastructuring is not only what leads to the creation of large systems designed and created centrally from above, but can also consist of the creation of a spontaneous infrastructure from below, constituted by products and services originally designed with different purposes. We will see later that to go from the city of distances to that of proximity, both types of processes are necessary.

That said, speaking of infrastructure and its design, we need to carefully consider what it does and does not make it possible to do, and how and to what extent it orients our action. This reference can appear obvious, but it is not. The specificity of an infrastructure is that of operating while being as invisible as possible. This, because attention is concentrated on what it makes possible. But in any event, an infrastructure does not make it possible to do everything, and not everything it permits is equally easy to do. The fact is that, based on how it was constructed, and thus how it was designed, each infrastructure incorporates knowledge and values that, consciously or not, were introduced by the person who designed it. It invites us to act freely, but adopting the modalities proposed and within the field of possibility that is inscribed in its very characteristics.

To speak of all of this, we could use the word "affordance."[6] Originally, this word indicated the way the physical features of an object suggest to the user how the object is to be used.[7] Then, the meaning was extended to what an infrastructure makes possible, and how. In our case, the affordance that interests us is that which invites people to encounter each other, collaborate, and construct new social forms. It should be noted that, in both meanings, the original one and the extended one, the concept refers to a strongly relational quality: an "invitation" is something whose meaning depends both on who does it (in our case, the infrastructure) and who receives it (in our case, those who, thanks to this infrastructure, could encounter each other, preserve, and construct communities).

To make those ideas more concrete, we can give the example of social infrastructure conceived precisely to support and orient the initiatives and enterprises that are widespread in society, and with this, to solve problems in proximity by activating the formation of communities of place.

The example is what in Italy is called the "Regulation on collaboration between citizens and administration":[8] a local administration draws up a list of unused areas and buildings, for which coalitions of citizens (and also associations, social enterprises, and private enterprises) can propose ideas on what to do with them and commit to doing it. This is a clear example of infrastructure that was produced to support local social innovations, and at the same time, bring a bit of order to the self-infrastructuring that such social innovations had generated until then (finding the way to use spaces and buildings outside of what was officially regulated up to that time). We can add that these collaboration regulations are formulated so as to include orientations for those who propose a project and the commitments to be assumed by the administration. This is obviously affordance of this particular social infrastructure: by indicating the criteria of acceptability of the proposals and the modes of participation, the regulation stimulates and sustains the creativity and enterprise of citizens, orienting them towards the production of urban common goods. In other words, this infrastructure, like all similar ones, incorporates in its nature the value of active citizenship and citizenship of common goods, and despite not imposing solutions, invites those who use it to operate freely but adopting the same values. Using the words of Dimitris Papadopoulos, social infrastructures of this type are transparent spaces, unnoticed, but which always incorporate political practice into their own functioning.[9]

4.2   From the city of distances to the city of proximity

Designing to bring close also requires transforming existing technical and social infrastructure, thus modifying the urban ecosystem as a whole and in the different systems of proximity of which it consists. This is certainly not an easy task; but in this case as well, social innovation helps us.

Carefully observing the examples proposed in the previous chapters, we see that, in starting from where we are now (the city of distances) to go where we would like to go (the city of proximity) what needs to be done is the composition of five actions: *localize* (bring services and activities close to citizens), *socialize* (favor the construction of communities); *include* (extend the network of actors involved); *diversify* (involve initially unforeseen actors); and *coordinate* (horizontally connect different areas of intervention).

These five actions (that we find in all cases of mature urban social innovation) are not to be considered as successive phases of a process, but as necessary components, although not necessarily present in the same way and order in each project. Let us take a closer look.

Localize: bring services and work opportunities close to citizens

This action consists of reorganizing the service, administrative, and production systems, going from vertical and hierarchical models to distributed models, bringing its nodes into the citizens' systems of proximity. In practice, as already said, the goal is to create a condition of functional proximity in which each citizen finds the services they need daily as well as a job opportunity, just a few minutes from home by foot. This idea is not new per se. In the past, similar distributed organizational forms clashed with the opposing (and dominant) forms, that in the name of efficiency, proposed vertical systems and large concentrations of activities. Today, though, the picture has changed: connectivity, digital platforms, and miniaturization means that distributed systems are much easier to create, generating more effective, resilient, and – potentially – democratic systems (see Box 1.3).

Designing to localize thus means adopting a distributed model, "vertically" shifting the productive activities and services towards the end users. In the cases discussed in the previous chapters (the neighborhoods of Barcelona in Chapter 2, and the WeMi program of Milan in Chapter 3), we have seen how care activities for the elderly have been localized, with advantages for both those who receive the service, and for those who provide it, as well as for the city as a whole. Obviously, the road to follow is, case by case, more or less practicable according to the type of activity and the context: localizing activities of social assistance can be more reasonable than localizing specialist medical services; bringing office activities into proximity can be easier than bringing productive activities into proximity. Furthermore, in some cases, it is not about localizing, but maintaining and regenerating activities of proximity that exist but are in crisis, such as neighborhood shops. For all cases, a new economy of proximity is to be constructed, which has greater possibility of success, where the system of proximity in which it operates is sufficiently rich and diversified (such as in the examples of Barcelona and Milan). Thus, even if cases like these proposed are important because they indicate the path to follow, the great challenge of livable proximity – and the localization of the activities and services that must sustain it – is in all those areas in which such urban quality is not present or is very low.

Socialize: favor the construction of communities

This action consists of promoting and supporting the construction of communities around themes of localized services: communities of care, educational communities, work communities, cultural communities, and so on. The motivation for doing this comes from the recognition of the importance of the relational dimension of proximity. Without this aspect, the localization we have mentioned could lead to a city of services distributed based on the provider-customer relationship. As we have seen (in Chapter 3), this corresponds to a careless society unable to address the dimensions and variety of problems we must face. On the other hand, from what we mentioned in the previous chapters, we know that socialization, understood as the creation of communities, cannot be designed directly. What can be done, and must be done, is to create a favorable environment in which sociality and community can emerge and last over time.

Designing to socialize means contributing to the production of this favorable environment. In practice, this implies changing the nature of the services, reorganizing them in a collaborative form and conceiving them as systems enabling the new communities we would like to see emerge. The proposal of circles of care in England, the territorial reorganization of home services in Barcelona, and the WeMi spaces hosted in cafés or other meeting places in Milan, all go in the same direction: transform what could have been a traditional medical or social service into an activity enabling new communities of care. Analogous considerations could apply to other areas of intervention, considering the possibility to construct educational communities around a school; food communities around a market or shops in proximity; reading communities around a library, and so on. As we will see in more detail later, socialization, intended in this sense, is a fundamental action to make the other four possible.

Include: extend the network of actors involved

This action consists of opening the communities so as to make them interesting and welcoming for many people, incuding those who are very different in terms of roles, age, and social class.[10] To do so, however, is not easy. Constructing a new community requires time, energy, and attention. Not coincidentally, those who dedicate themselves to such a task are often considered "social heroes." This heroic character, though, can make access difficult for others, who are potentially interested, but who for various reasons, do not have a similar availability of time, energy, or motivation.

Designing to include means taking that difficulty into account operating in two areas. The first implies introducing, from the beginning, goals and rules that favor openness and the variety of the participants. For example, a community of care can aim to include marginalized people, or a cohousing initiative can set the rule of forming a heterogeneous group by age, social status, and ethnicity. The second area on which to operate is the development of enabling platforms that, by reducing the time, energy, and attention required to participate in the life of the community, lower the entry threshold, and make the community itself welcoming for a greater number of participants. To this intervention, that operates principally on the functional dimension of the platform, another must be added, that is just as important, that acts on the field of meaning and motivation, to make the sense of these communities clear to a vaster and more diversified public.

Diversify: involve initially unforeseen actors

This action implies integrating in the construction and life of a community some initially unforeseen figures, who bring the energy and skills that become necessary step by step. These new members of the community can have different profiles: experts, associations, representatives of local entities, and social or market enterprises, that in various ways can be involved in the themes that the community finds itself addressing. The interesting aspect of this type of inclusion is that it brings to the community, and thus to the group that addresses a given theme, human and material resources that in a non-innovative vision would not have been present.

Designing to diversify thus implies a redefinition of the original system (that could be the system of social services, health, and the local administration) to integrate it with people and entities that originally were not included. For example, as we have seen in Chapter 3, cafés that, by also becoming places for encounters for social services, de facto become part of them; laundromats that, by offering work spaces, de facto become coworking locations; newsstands that, by offering administrative services for the City, de facto become an extension of the public administration; and so on. It is clear that this operation requires creativity and strategic vision, but it is also made possible by the fact that the community to diversify refers to a rich and diversified system of proximity; in other words, there cannot be shops that become antennas for social services, if there are no neighborhoods shops anymore.

Coordinate: connect different areas of intervention horizontally

The communities that we have discussed to this point are constructed around specific themes that, in turn, refer to different and separate systems of services (health, social services, school, green, mobility, etc.). It is important that they connect horizontally with other communities that, in the same place, have been constructed around other themes. By doing so, intersecting and interweaving with each other, and operating in the same neighborhood, these communities can coordinate by making their respective activities more effective and improving the quality of life that they propose together. At the same time, these intersections can lead to the emergence of a system of proximity that is more interconnected and a community of place that, by including and coordinating the various projects and communities it consists of, can improve the quality and efficacy of their whole.

Designing to coordinate means connecting and locally integrating both project-based communities and service systems. This local coordination can take place in different ways. All of them, though, are likely to be successful if the previous four steps have been implemented; that is, if the service systems have been localized, if they have contributed to creating communities, and if the communities that have been formed are inclusive and diversified. When this has happened, local coordination no longer risks being perceived as an administrative act from above, but emerges from the practices of people (citizens, experts, administrators) who live and operate in the same neighborhood and who, if they want, can easily encounter each other, even at a café without an appointment.

4.3   Stimuli and attractors of the social conversation

The five steps just described can be seen as guidelines: what needs to be done to create systems of proximity inhabited by communities of place. As anticipated, their sequence and their weight depend on the context, i.e. on the state of the pre-existing systems of proximity and communities. We now add that, in any event, the second action (socializing, intended as favoring the construction of communities) is the crucial one. In fact, to implement the previous steps, i.e. to include and diversify, it is necessary for a community to exist, or at least to be under construction. That is not all: the first step, that of localization of the activities and services, although it can be achieved as the result of an autonomous decision by the entities in charge, can also be facilitated and made more effective by the existence of local communities involved in the initiative. On the other hand, conceived as an action to carry out, that is, as something to design and implement, socializing to create communities is the most delicate and difficult of the five. We know, in fact, that what we want to obtain cannot be directly designed: the relationships which are the basis of the communities that we would like to see born do not take place by decree. We also know, however, that the conditions can be created to make encounters possible and probable (encounters that can evolve into conversations, collaboration, and thus communities).

Finally, again as a whole, the five steps described are those that lead to having everything that is needed for people to be able to dance, but in order for the dancing to actually begin, music is needed. Outside of the metaphor, something is needed that can stimulate and orient the encounters and conversations.

Observing the projects proposed in the previous chapters, we see that, indeed, many of them have produced something tangible that in turn has stimulated encounters, conversations, and thus empathy, mutual trust, the ability to collaborate, and shared visions. In brief, the products of these projects have functioned as enzymes able to activate and catalyze social resources,[11] and they have done it in two ways: stimulating conversations and favoring their convergence.

The first mode involves placing products or events that offer occasions for encounters and conversations. These can be artistic performances or neighborhood parties, or also texts, images, or films. They can also be products capable of stimulating a discussion. Each of these interventions, including those conceived to perform a function, has a story to tell, and for this reason can have a relational capacity. They can be chairs placed in the middle of Las Ramblas in Barcelona to break the flow of tourists and invite them to a conversation with the residents; the decorations for a neighborhood party, to create a discussion on its identity; or even the aesthetic quality of a center for the elderly, that can lead to speaking of the dignity of aging. When this happens, when these conversations take place, it means that the artifacts that have triggered them have also operated as *relational objects*,[12] and must also be assessed from this standpoint. Obviously, there is no formula to say how and when the result of a project can play (also) this role. The possibility that this will take place certainly depends on the sensitivity of the designer, but also on the availability and reactivity of the possible interlocutors.

The other role, that is complementary to the previous one, is that of helping different social actors to construct a common vision and orient their actions in that direction. The process that leads to this result can certainly take place in a non-organized manner, thanks to a rich social conversation able to lead the participants to converge in the same direction. However, this social conversation can be stimulated and its convergence assisted thanks to some artifacts: communicative artifacts that bring attention, and discussion, to one or more possible futures.[13] This means that a practicable vision is proposed of how things could be, given certain conditions; that is, of how that vision could be transformed into practice. As for relational objects, this vision can be offered by an artistic performance, a neighborhood festival, a text, a video, or an image, on the condition that, in this case, they contribute to producing an idea of how things could be.[14] This aim can also be obtained thanks to the use of tools specifically conceived for this purpose: *functioning prototypes* and *design-orienting scenarios.*

The former show us tangibly how certain aspects of the overall vision of which they are a part could truly function, thus making it more concrete.[15] Functioning prototypes can be designed ad hoc, but not only; initiatives that someone has created due to their own motivations can also function this way, if once realized they function as concrete and valid examples for everyone of how things could be done. Thus we can say that the social innovations we have dealt with to this point can be shared as functioning prototypes of a vision of city and society in opposition to the dominant ones. In fact, in addition to having offered precise solutions to specific problems, having shown concrete examples of how things could be, they have become the object of other conversations on what to do. And they have contributed to making other projects converge in the same direction. By doing so, they are to be considered in the same manner as contents of an emerging scenario of possible and sustainable cities.

This last observation leads us to the second family of attractors: design-orienting scenarios. A formal definition of this term is as follows: a design-orienting scenario is a communicative artifact that, by activating the social conversation, favors the convergence of different actors and different projects. Operationally, it is composed of an overall vision divided into specific goals, and by the tools used to reach them.[16] In our case, the proposal of the city of proximity is intrinsically a scenario because it is based on a vision that has been constructed in many years of social innovation in the cities, and that acquires concrete form precisely from the existence of the functioning prototypes that this same innovation has produced (and that, we have said, have given a tangible idea of how some aspects of daily life could be in the city of proximity). On the other hand, this scenario can offer a framework of meaning in which the various social innovations (those that have contributed to constructing it, and those that will come later) can find their place also as pieces of a mosaic that, as a whole, produce an image on a greater scale; which is precisely what is needed more than ever today.

4.4   Communities of place as an interweave of projects

To this point, we have defined the steps to take and some tools to develop to go from the city of distances to that of proximity. Now, to take another step forward in this same direction, it is necessary to change the point of view and look at things from inside and close up.

To do so here, we will consider two cases from Milan and we will seek the help of two friends who are among their promoters. Thanks to them, we will be able to discuss what it truly means to design to be close; in particular what it means to construct a community of place (with reference to a neighborhood, in the case considered) and how a community evolves and transforms to last over time without losing its initial qualities (we will refer here to an experience of collaborative social housing).

In the previous chapters (in particular Chapter 1 and Chapter 3) we defined what characterizes contemporary communities of place: they are groups of people with a common interest for where they live, who collaborate in various ways to care for it. Now we can resume the discussion going a bit deeper as regards their nature and relationship with the system of proximity to which they refer. To speak of this concretely, we will describe the experience of a neighborhood in Milan, called NoLo, and the story of one of its protagonists.

Example 7   *North of Loreto, a neighborhood*
as a project-based incubator
by *Davide Fassi*
(Associate Professor of the Department of Design,
Milan Polytechnic University)

NoLo (North of Loreto) is the name given to an area of the city of Milan that covers a territory that counts approximately 25,000 inhabitants. Considered the periphery for years, not so much for its geographic position, but because of the problems linked to quality of life and the spaces it consists of, the area has historically been home to various migratory flows, from both domestic and international sources. Over the decades of the last century, NoLo took in cultures, traditions, behavior, and customs that strongly characterized its social fabric[17] and generated a perception of the neighborhood as dangerous, difficult, poor, and needy.[18] Today the foreign population is over 34 percent of the total, compared to an average of 19 percent for the city as a whole. While on the one hand this heterogeneity has a rich potential for social contamination, on the other it still indicates a strong identification of the single communities to the detriment of true integration, which however is slowly emerging. For a few years now, the area has in fact been the center of a process of urban and social transformation that includes not only the opening of new service activities for citizens, galleries, and creative studios, but also the spontaneous aggregation of the residents around different online and offline activities. There is an intensive activity of collaboration and encounters between the residents, which is reflected in the more historic and formal forms that refer to the variegated world of Milan's associations, but also in other new and informal forms such as the NoLo Social District,[19] an expanded social street that counts more than 10,000 members and that facilitates a process of knowledge and help in the small problems of daily life between neighbors, that most of the time leads to offline activities of consolidation of the relationship or to project ideas.[20]

Before being identified with this name, NoLo had an identity linked to small portions of its territory, characterized by a very specific form of association life, with the participation of groups of people with goals firmly linked to the care, preservation, and improvement of these places and their specific characteristics.[21] The interpretation we can give to its community today, on the other hand, outlines a constellation of interconnected initiatives, characterized by a group of people who are concentrated around one or more projects, generating a neighborhood social system and having the goal of improving the area. The community has been activated only recently, but has unique characteristics that can be viewed through the projects around which the communities are formed.

Those projects also include the work carried out with the residents of the neighborhood by POLIMI DESIS Lab, a design research group for social innovation of the Department of Design of the Milan Polytechnic University. Since 2016, POLIMI DESIS Lab has launched a series of research and teaching activities in the field, tapping into the proactive nature of the local community in projects regarding spaces and services for the territory. Certain solutions have been attempted to strengthen the creative identity of the neighborhood and to enhance the artisanal tradition and commercial vocation of the fabric of streets and roads present, through actions that have involved people (artists and creatives who were already present and also newcomers, local shopkeepers, private citizens, and the formal or informal groups of which they are a part) and places (the streets, covered city market, and squares).

The distinctive features of these projects clarify some characteristics that emerge from the initiatives themselves.

1. *Adopt digital tools for socialization – NoLo Social District (2016)*
   The need to generate relations with neighbors and the needs linked to the resolution of small daily problems have found a digital home in the neighborhood

Facebook group. The variety of age groups and the high number of its members provide a picture of a strong vocation to use the digital tool as a first form of acquaintance, despite the physical proximity of the members of the group.

2. *Use public space – Neighborhood breakfast (2016)*
This was the first socialization activity born inside of the NoLo Social District, when two women who were neighbors set up a table and a pair of chairs on a small portion of the sidewalk to share coffee and cookies with the passers-by. In a short period of time, it became a regular appointment that lasted for over three years, and allowed many residents of the neighborhood to meet each other in person, going from an online relationship, to an offline one.

3. *Modify public space – Mobì Project (2017), Open streets (2020)*
The Mobì Project was created at the time of the participatory budget of the City of Milan in 2018, inside the NoLo Social District, with the idea of developing a proposal for making use of the funds made available by the city administration to improve portions of public space. About fifty residents from three associations presented a project that foresaw paths for slow and safe mobility. Although the idea did not win the competition for funding, the City decided to adopt it as a strategic plan for mobility in the neighborhood, and in April 2019, began to experiment with its efficacy, opening three work sites in two years. Open streets is an applied research project conducted in 2020 by POLIMI DESIS Lab that continued within the Mobì Project, transforming portions of streets for vehicles (parking places and areas), into areas for people, equipped with street furniture in collaboration with the shopkeepers in the area.

4. *Communicate and talk about the neighborhood – Radio NoLo and Giranolo (2017)*
A way to communicate the neighborhood's new identity has been found through these two projects. Radio NoLo is the web-radio in the neighborhood that, with a volunteer staff of approximately eighty people, currently produces sixteen programs that talk about the neighborhood. Weekly news programs, analysis, and entertainment are recording the changes underway. While the accounts given by the radio are online, the reality of Giranolo exists that brings it offline. Also born within the NoLo Social District, the group consists of volunteers who organize free tours of the neighborhood to point out its architecture, history, and the people who have lived there.

5. *Implement and host welfare solutions – WeMi and the Qubì network (2019)*
The WeMi spaces are points for encounters and orientation in which, thanks to specialized operators, the welfare solutions most suited for people in dif-

ficulty are identified. The project was created by the City of Milan, but has found a location in the neighborhood in one of the places regenerated in recent years by a group of residents, a former artisanal workshop that currently hosts a cultural association.

The Qubì network has brought together fifteen groups active in the world of associations and volunteer work, thanks to funding from a bank foundation (Fondazione Cariplo) with the goal of implementing solutions for the education of minors (after-school, training courses, and aggregation activities), food assistance and health and well-being (events dedicated to personal care, medical visits, food advice, and health care).

6. *Combat food poverty – Spesa Sospesa (2020)*
   With the first lockdown due to the Covid-19 emergency in March 2020, an initiative developed by two residents of the neighborhood led to a project to help people with financial difficulties. Through registration on a digital platform, neighbors can make a monetary donation to pay for groceries that are purchased by a group of volunteers and delivered to needy families that in turn have indicated their needs by registering on the site. In a short period of time a system of solidarity was generated that has collected 30,000 euros and reached over 600 families. The idea was then revived during the second lockdown, in November 2020, introducing the requirement to buy the goods in neighborhood stores, so as to help the small shopkeepers and the local economy as well.

7. *Strengthen cultural activities – Arnold. Arte and design in NoLo (2017)*
   The neighborhood is the location of numerous artist ateliers, artisanal workshops, and creative enterprises, both recent and present historically. Despite being numerous, they are not places and professions known well by the residents of NoLo. In 2017, POLIMI DESIS Lab activated first a path to map these activities, and then a series of co-design activities. The goal has been to enhance that cultural wealth through a series of events inside 24 shops in the neighborhood that have hosted exhibits and talks by the artists involved.[22]

8. *Enhance the projects of the existing community – Off Campus NoLo (2018)*
   In the covered neighborhood market, after three years of teaching coordinated by the POLIMI DESIS Lab that produced various different scenarios of use, the City of Milan provided the administrative tools to assign unoccupied spaces for the creation of a research laboratory, Off Campus NoLo. This is an initiative by the Milan Polytechnic University to strengthen its presence in the city of Milan and the idea of a university that is more responsible, attentive to social challenges, and open and close to territories and communities, through

> the activation and facilitation of projects with existing local activities. In NoLo,
> it hosts an observatory on issues linked to the regeneration and reactivation
> of neighborhoods; teaching laboratories and workshops, seminars and les-
> sons open to the neighborhood, shows and exhibits, public events, and an
> open neighborhood archive.[23]

In recent years, a complex social dynamic has arisen in NoLo that has led to the creation of a new community of place, and at the same time, a renewed offer of activities and functions; that is, an increased diversification of the system of proximity.

The first and most evident characteristic of this community is its complexity, i.e. its emergence from the interweave of a variety of groups, each of which works on a project. These are people who, having brought into focus a theme of common interest and having identified problems and opportunities in the neighborhood, work to make something happen. Each of these project-based communities has its own autonomy. And the same is true for the projects around which they are formed. At the same time, the different projects and different communities are connected with each other in many ways. It is precisely the sum of these projects and their interconnections that generates the community of place as an entity that is both complex and unitary at the same time.

Another aspect that characterizes these communities of place is thus given by the type of projects – and thus of project-based communities – on which they are constructed. The projects can in fact tend to obtain a well-defined result (transforming a square so that children can play there, organizing neighborhood tours, creating slow mobility paths), or they can aim to connect people, operating as platforms for activities and projects to be defined (as in the cited cases of the NoLo Social District and Radio NoLo). Thus dual nature of the projects also reflects on what the communities around them generate, and that therefore, in turn, can be *targeted* (i.e. defined by a precise result they obtain to intend) or *connective* (that aim to offer platforms open to various possibilities). It should be added that the community of place that results is also a project-based community. But in this case, it is a project that emerges from the intersection of many different micro-projects, whose overall goal is the improvement of the neighborhood, and thus the system of proximity that characterizes it. For this, precisely because it is based on multiple operational projects that enrich the system of proximity with activities and functions, this same project-based community is also an agent that regenerates diversified proximity.

A third aspect that characterizes the community concerns the variety of participants, meaning who is involved and how. Here as well, everything depends on the number of projects. Since they regard different themes, and since each of them can involve a different group of people, overall they produce a community of place that is very articulated and diversified. And that's not all: the concrete and operational nature of the theme around which each project is constructed means that the participants can agree on the project but have different opinions on other themes, or represent social and ethnic groups that, otherwise, would be unlikely to connect with each other. Obviously, all of this cannot guarantee avoiding the social uniformity of the participants; however, for the reasons recalled previously, it is less likely that this uniformity will appear.

Linked to the previous theme is another distinguishing aspect that is useful to recall, which is how different projects intersect, connect, and in some cases, are coordinated. These interactions of coordination can take on different forms. The most elementary is given by the fact that the people themselves, being residents in the same neighborhood, can participate in multiple projects, thus de facto acting as a link between them. Another form of connection is given by the intersections and overlaps that are created between projects that are independent but that operate in the same neighborhood. In concrete terms, this imposes the need for interaction, and in some cases, coordination (for example, in the case of NoLo, the projects relating to safety and children's play are linked to those regarding green areas, as well as those relating to business, the use of public spaces, and the limiting of vehicle traffic). Lastly, there can be a structured connection, implemented through dedicated tools, such as specific coordination bodies (a neighborhood association, for example), or, as in the case of NoLo, by creating common platforms (the NoLo Social District) or tools for information and conversation (Radio No- Lo, the neighborhood radio station).

Finally, there is the most important aspect to guarantee that these communities are able to regenerate themselves, and thus last in time: the multiplicity of forms of participation that they allow for, and the possibility to modify them over time. The request in terms of effort varies according to the type of project (as already said, there are different themes for different interests, and there are projects that, by their nature, are more demanding, while there are others that are less so) but the necessary participation can be very different even within a single project, where there is room for more active people (who operate as a *project coalition*,[24] with the responsibility and management of the project), but also for those who participate only in specific co-design and co-production activities; and also all of those who simply participate in some events, supporting the project's values, and thus feeling like they too are a part of the community. Moreover, since there are multiple projects and they take place with different timeframes, the participation of each one in the community can vary over time. The community of place that is produced is in turn open and flexible: everyone can find the role they prefer on the theme they care most about, and at the moment most favorable for them.

The theme of participation, and thus of the time, attention, and level of enthusiasm it entails, is inevitably related to that of the natural fatigue that this participation can generate in the single individuals and in the community as a whole. Thus it is necessary to focus the discussion on these new communities from a longer temporal perspective than we have adopted to this point. Specifically, it is necessary to go from a quasi-synchronous vision (the photograph of what is happening) to a diachronic vision (the film of what has happened over the years). When we began to deal with these themes, the second vision was not present, because the cases it could refer to were almost all new. This is no longer the case, and it is possible – and very important, although still not very common – to see how things have evolved in time; how from the initial heroic phase, in which the initiatives were driven by a coherent group of enthusiastic citizens, the phase of normality – and fatigue – is reached regarding the management of everything that must be done from day to day to regenerate this community, maintaining its original values over time and reproducing the complexity and diversity of the system of proximity on which those values are based.

4.5   Construction and regeneration

To take a step in the direction just indicated, we will use another example: *Cenni di Cambiamento* is a project realized in Milan in 2013, in Via Cenni, by the Lombardy Real Estate Fund and the Social Housing Foundation (FHS). This case will help us get an up-close view not only of how a project-based community is constructed, but also of how it evolves over time. There are two reasons for the choice of this experience as a point of reference. The first is that it is a project that already has a sufficiently long history, and thus it has necessarily passed from the start-up phase to the subsequent operational phase. Furthermore, and not less important, the continuous work of monitoring and assistance carried out by FHS allows for knowing what has actually happened in recent years.

Example 8 **_Collaborative living at maturity: the experience_**
of the social housing foundation in Milan
by _Giordana Ferri_
(Executive Director of the Social Housing Foundation)

The collaborative social housing interventions[25] promoted by the Social Housing Foundation offer a collaborative living solution that includes price-controlled dwellings, primarily through leases, and the opportunity to share spaces and services with neighbors in which to carry out all of the activities linked to daily life, without necessarily having in one's own house or resources everything that is needed for such activities (for example, think of sharing spaces for children to play, holding a cultural event, organizing a buying group, making tomato purée for the winter, repairing an object, cooking for many people, etc.).

Fondazione Housing Sociale was born in 2004 with this goal: to develop the Social Housing project of the Cariplo Foundation,[26] carrying out social initiatives and experimenting with new approaches to interventions through design that integrates architectural, economic, and social contents; in short, identifying in collaborative housing the model to adopt for the development of social housing. The heart of this activity consists of enabling people, tenants' groups, and even more so, future tenants, to construct their neighborhood, making themselves available for the platforms.

Offering platforms means giving access to: tools to facilitate organization and communication, spaces (beyond strictly residential spaces), a structured process, resources and knowledge that accelerate the process of forming the group and the provision of services. The methodology adopted to work with the residents is strictly linked to _co-design_: we ask them to come up with and manage the activities, and we help them to implement the project, in a short time and with minimum effort. To do so we have conceived dedicated tools with which to design and prototype the activities, a platform to manage the projects and facilitate communication between the tenants, tutorials to effectively and efficiently carry out the approved initiatives and to structure their governance (an application is available to the tenants of all of the collaborative housing interventions carried out by the Fund, allowing them to manage the common spaces and share the projects).

In general terms, the aim of the intervention is the implementation of the services and the ways of living in the common spaces proposed by the residents. Concretely, the process begins approximately six months prior to the arrival of the first tenants and is concluded a year after the residents have entered their houses. The ultimate goal is to enable the tenants to plan the use of the common spaces at their disposal, and to define the rules that will govern them. During the process, the tenants decide and begin to develop the activities chosen, establish and adopt governance, structure an organization, set up the spaces, and get to know each other through parties, encounters, and other occasions for sharing.

In the end it may happen that the residents, who have carried out all of the demanding activity of organization and taken delivery of the common spaces, experience a drop in energy level compared to what they had at in the initial phase. This is the phase of entry into a sort of new normal: the shift from an exceptional situation, needed to "get it moving," to that of day-by-day management. At this point the project needs a readaptation that allows everyone to continue in a dimension of normality. Two questions are essentially posed: the preservation of the human resources necessary to carry out the projects (the rate of abandonment can be high, due to the natural evolution over time of the needs that had initially stimulated participation), and the optimization of the organization, that must weigh as little as possible compared to the development of the contents of the project.

One of the collaborative living interventions carried out by the funds belonging to the *Fondo Investimenti per l'Abitare (FIA)* is *Cenni di Cambiamento*,[27] that was carried out and is owned by the Lombardy Real Estate Fund, managed by Redo sgr. This is a residential intervention, carried out in 2013, consisting of 122 dwellings, offered for lease at a fixed, "social" price, and leased with a future sale clause. In addition to the residence, the complex contains collective services and spaces, neighborhood shops and local urban services. Since the spring of 2016, Cenni has also hosted the *Mare Culturale Urbano* (Urban Cultural Sea) project,[28] centered on innovation, urban regeneration, and social inclusion through spaces for art, training, work, and free time. On September 28, 2014, a residents' association was also founded, *Officina Gabetti 15*, that has the aim of promoting the participation of everyone in activities, events, initiatives, and moments of aggregation, sharing ideas, means, and experiences. In October 2015, the association began using the common spaces of the Cenni project under a gratuitous use agreement.

In this intervention, four years later, the tenants asked themselves how they could have overcome the organizational problems that often weighed on the people who were more available, and that were endangering the project. They found a hybrid, win-win solution, that consists of involving some non-profit entities that revolve around the project in the direct management of the spaces and logistics. In exchange, these entities use the spaces for their own activities for free in the hours when they are normally empty (for example, in the morning).

 This example indicates a path for the evolution of the practices of collaborative living in the passage from the initial setup phase to that of long-term functioning; that is, from the heroic phase to that of relative normality.

The fundamental suggestion that has emerged from the Cenni experience is the need to open the community of residents to the neighborhood, a *conditio sine qua non* for the project to be able to last over time. The level of turnover ensures the constant presence of people willing to contribute with enthusiasm over time. This aspect, that is fundamental in volunteer-based collaborative initiatives, is not as obvious in a residential project. In fact, a residential community strongly identifies itself with the space it occupies, a space that by its nature is limited, as is the community that lives in it. This limitation, that represents one of the fundamental elements of the collaborative residential project, can at the same time constitute the largest obstacle to its growth.

To summarize: how is it possible to guarantee the survival of the group through the natural and cyclical injection of new energy and resources? How can the collaborative residential project not be limited to just the scale of the building?

As suggested above, we can answer these questions by opening up to a larger basin of people.

Collaborative residential interventions could be transformed into neighborhood hubs and share spaces and tools with all entities (for profit and non-profit), thus deriving economic resources to compensate those who deal with the logistics and organization, or bartering spaces for services. This means imagining that the spaces and collaborative activities are destined not only to a single building, but at least to a portion of the neighborhood. We can thus imagine having in the neighborhood self-managed functions that, as in collaborative living, represent the expansion of the home, but also that group people on the basis of not only physical, but elective geographies. This is already happening spontaneously: think of the social streets and social districts that create cohesion around the desire to construct a neighborhood on the basis of common activities. Those activities could use the spaces and instruments already in use in profit or low-profit initiatives. By way of example: structured and spontaneous coworking, revitalized shops with collective functions, and commercial activities open to mixed and collective use. Obviously, the entrepreneurial activities to which they refer are not just any organizations. Many are examples of work, residential, or service projects that see sharing as a solid response to new needs. The places in which they take place are normally characterized by mixed uses, with the prevalence of the dimension of sharing spaces and services (in this case on a paid basis).

> When this happens, as we were saying, a win-win situation arises: for for-profit entities, the possibility to integrate local groups means having a strong urban presence and potential roots for their establishment; collaborative activists gain the opportunity to have spaces available for their projects without running costs; and both have the possibility of a greater impact on the choices and development of the territory.
>
> These structures can become sensitive and vital nodes in the city, because they are lived in by communities that are conscious, receptive, and interacting. They can become an engine for the start of processes of urban generation and construction of social fabric.
>
> This is only the beginning of a reflection that is based in part on the observation of already-existing phenomena, and in part on projects underway that draw indications from them. Certainly, collaborative projects, like all other projects, must be characterized today by a strongly adaptive and constructive spirit that allows them to change and find new solutions each time.

Today, the via Cenni project is a place and a community. The place is a complex of social housing units. The community consists of the residents, but also, as we will see, of outside persons, who have interests, skills, and capabilities, linked to the projects that have gradually been activated and developed.

Eight years after the beginning of this story, the overall picture of via Cenni shows us a place in which, in addition to the dwellings (122 of them) there are shared spaces among the residents (a living room, a kitchen, a play area, gardens, and four shared terraces) and those in which seven business activities are hosted, as well as the offices of associations and cultural and social enterprises. In addition, during 2019 (i.e. the last year before the pandemic) 154 activities were organized at via Cenni, considering both those dedicated only to the tenants and those that were public and open to the neighborhood.

What this picture of the place cannot show us is the dynamic network of relations that has kept, and still keeps all of this alive, i.e. the via Cenni community. To see it, we need to get close to it. Actually, we need to go inside the community itself and its dynamics.

A community such as via Cenni is not born by chance, but because an idea is proposed, along with the tools to create it; the idea of a mode of collaborative living that, functioning as a stimulus and an attractor, generated the motivation to participate and allowed for the convergence towards a shared vision. At the same time, the tools were provided (a method and a supporting platform) that made it practically possible for people to meet, exchange experiences, and learn to collaborate; and by so doing, to become a community.

The community we are speaking of was formed by co-designing spaces, services, and modes of action. In doing this, it defined in a shared manner the meaning to give to the type of collaborative living to be created. Not only the tenants participated in this process of coming closer, but the FHS team of experts did as well. These experts are to be seen as active members of the community itself: this point is very important and we will return to it later. For now it is sufficient to recall that the communities to which we refer include all of those that, with different roles and skills, participate collaboratively in the definition and realization of a project. In this case, what was formed is an expert community, made up of the tenants of via Cenni, as well as the entities that participated and participate in generating the result to be reached together. It should be noted and highlighted that, since the different phases of the co-design and co-production processes require different skills, the community that emerges varies over time according to needs and opportunities. This variability of the community, this characteristic of variable geometry, is not a problem. Rather, today, given the fluid character of the entire society, it is precisely this opening and flexibility that make a community contemporary.

The shared vision of collaborative living around which the via Cenni community was formed was not a remake of a pre-existing model; it was the result of an original co-design activity that, from an initial idea and the interaction between different points of view and ideas of what to do and how, led to a shared and practicable vision, specific to the place and people involved. The interaction between an initial stimulus (in this case provided by the FHS team) and the conversation within the group that was being formed, is what created the sense of "collective ownership" of the project and the recognition by everyone of being part of a group and having shared ideas on collaborative living. The vision that was thus produced made it possible to give coherence to everything that the group itself was able to do.

As a whole, all of this can be seen as the construction of a system of *hyper-localized* proximity, where the prefix "hyper" has a dual meaning: it is hyper-local because the ideas and practices on which it is based are specific to a well-defined place and group of actors; at the same time, it is hyper-open because it is a localization born and developed in relation to ideas and sensitivities of a general nature: the environmental and social value of what is being done, the perception that one's own action resonates with other analogous actions that, together, contribute to producing a shared idea of city and society.

That is not all: by defining services and spaces to be shared and agreeing on rules for use and apportionment of management activities, the community that has been built has transformed these spaces and services into *common goods* (it can be useful to recall that common goods are not only resources to be shared, but also the rules that the community which is the principal beneficiary of these common goods establishes to guarantee their duration in time and equity in sharing). We can thus say that in a case such as this one, a system of proximity is created that also includes a set of common goods; and that these goods, like all common goods, are as precious as they are delicate and require care over time. In short, the case of via Cenni tells us that it is possible to create the conditions for the activation – in this case in a hyper-local form – of a virtuous circle between community, collaboration, care, and common goods.

4.6   From the heroic phase to transformative normality

What we have described for via Cenni here, is by now an archive picture. It is what happened years ago. Now we need to see the film of what happened afterwards.

In order to last over time, the via Cenni community, like all similar communities, has had to continuously recreate the conditions for its own existence; an activity of *regeneration* that in turn has required – and still requires – creativity, design thinking, and enterprise; and thus time, attention, and care. And this, in a super-individualized society, in a city of disposability and connected solitude, means going against the grain, which is certainly not easy. Yet in this case, they succeeded, and the via Cenni community can be seen as a double miracle. The first miracle is what we have described to this point: people and families who did not know each other decided and were able to become a community of tenants (and not simply a condominium). The second is that this community has lasted, and still lasts, in time.

The double miracle can be explained by observing the generative interaction that has been created between the FHS support team and the tenants (starting from when the latter were not yet tenants, but only people who intended to become tenants). We will not retrace the whole story here (which however is well documented in various FHS publications[29]). Rather, we will isolate some of the lessons we can draw for the purposes of our reflection on proximity.

What this hypothetical film on via Cenni could show us is the contemporary construction of a community, a shared vision, and a way of doing things. And then, their evolution, without interruption, into an activity of management that, in turn, as we will see, is a continuous activity of regeneration. So it is necessary to see how the initial phase evolved and what was done when the abundant initial energy and enthusiasm were exhausted, and it became necessary to shift to the continuous management of what had been started.

Returning to and generalizing what is described in Example 8, we notice that the shift from the startup phase to the continuous management phase required a series of projects aimed at addressing the problems that gradually arose, to dynamize the existing community and open it to new contributions. In short, projects to structure, reinvent, and open the community.

To be more precise: in order to reduce the burden of management on the tenants, procedures were simplified, digital management systems were introduced, and the figure of the social manager was created, a professional who, in addition to managing the property and facilitating the relations with the owners facilitates the sharing of the spaces and services and the organization of the common activities promoted by the tenants. In addition to these initiatives, that were important but consistent with every process of normalization, others were added, that were intertwined with the former, but derived from the recognized need to continue reinventing the community, i.e. to imagine and create new projects. These projects were of various kinds and had various goals (for example: offer new services or develop various cultural or sports initiatives), but all of them, being conceived and carried out in a collaborative fashion, led to regenerating the fabric of relations, and very pragmatically, to making new energies emerge: new active tenants who joined the original group and/or made natural turnover possible.

Alongside those initiatives of regeneration, there was another of fundamental importance, that we can call an initiative of *opening* and *diversification*: opening the community to other entities involved − or that could potentially be involved – in activities of common interest. In the case of via Cenni, this took place in two steps. The first was to grant the use of common spaces to non-profit associations during hours of lower traffic, in turn asking them to participate in the management (and by so doing, lessening the burden of this activity on the tenants). This first step showed the possibility to implement another step: that of including other neighborhood actors in the community as well, non-profit entities but also commercial businesses that operated from the standpoint of an economy of proximity. By moving in this direction, the point came where a new community and a new system of proximity was imagined: a community composed of a variety of actors who bring their diverse abilities, skills, and experiences; a system of proximity based on a complex economy, in which the volunteer actions of active citizens are linked to the paid actions of the social operator and the various types of exchanges that take place with the non-profit and commercial entities that decide to participate in the project.

This line of action, that was adopted for via Cenni but that would mature in other subsequent social housing interventions, is particularly significant for us, on a practical and socio-political level; on the practical level because it brings new social resources, and in some cases economic resources, to the community (for example, shops or coworking of proximity); on the socio-political level because it makes the opening of the community to the neighborhood concrete and operational. And there is more: this line of action tends to make the community and the spaces of via Cenni, respectively, an agent and a hub for urban regeneration on a broader scale: the promoters of a more diversified system of proximity on a functional level, and a richer one in terms of relationships.

The initiatives just outlined are what the case of via Cenni teaches us on the passage from the initial phase to that of management; a phase in which, for those who experience it, this collaborative mode of action becomes part of daily life (both due to what it offers in terms of functional and relational proximity, and for what it requires, in terms of attention, participation, and care). This is true even though, in reality, what it proposes continues to be a way of living that goes against the dominant trend.

Via Cenni and other similar interventions can thus be read as experiments in *transformative normality*, an expression we use to indicate a way of doing and thinking that, despite becoming normal for some people in a given place (i.e., normal for those who adopt it), is not at all normal for other people in other contexts.[30] In other words, transformative normality is the result of a mature social innovation that, regenerating itself over time, has transformed its system of proximity, without losing its social and environmental value. In our example, what FHS created at via Cenni and the subsequent interventions can be seen as a condition of normality because what it requires (the sharing of spaces and services, collaboration in their functioning, and feeling like part of a community) is part of the daily normality of residents, including those who, for various reasons, do not have much time and energy to invest. At the same time, it is a transformative normality because its way of functioning, conflicting with the dominant thinking and practices at the general level, contributes to the preparation of a broader systemic change. The same can be said for many other successful social innovations: a shared or community garden contributes to creating a more sustainable city, even though, being born in the framework of an agreement with local institutions (such as a Regulation of collaboration between citizens and administration[31]), no longer requiring social heroes to be cultivated, it can involve a higher number of gardening and urban horticulture enthusiasts. Similarly, a farmer's market contributes to the reorganization of the relationship between the city and countryside, even if it has evolved to the point of being easily managed by the farmers and accessible by the citizens.

These forms of normality are thus the concrete and daily expression of the fact that social innovations have matured generating a new social infrastructure capable of making accessible and durable practices that otherwise would be confined to the circle of those who have more motivation, time, and energy available.

It should also be said, though, that this form of normality, being a local and partial change of a system of proximity that continues to be immersed in a hostile environment, is a fragile normality, always at risk of skidding towards the closing of the small group in a battle against everyone else, or more frequently, towards a normalization that is no longer transformative; that is, a normalization in which, gradually, we lose sight of the values and behavior that initially made it a harbinger of sustainable ways of living. For this reason, when an initiative is able to generate a situation of transformative normality, it has a value that goes beyond that for the residents and the relevant neighborhood. It becomes a functioning prototype of a new way of living and being a city, an element of the scenario of the city of proximity.

4.7   Designing in proximity and for proximity

To recapitulate: NoLo speaks to us of the nature of communities of place, their emergence from a constellation of projects and communities that form around them, and thus of the way they construct the system of proximity in which they are located, enriching it with services and activities, transforming it into a diversified and relational system inhabited by a living and dynamic community that cares for it.

The via Cenni community becomes a part of this discussion by telling us that every project, and thus every project-based community, is the result of initiatives on a smaller scale, that go down to the level of the individual life projects of each single participant. Therefore, to make the overall project last in time, it is necessary to develop forms of regeneration that allow the people already involved (in this case, the tenants) to renew their interest, but also, if and when they want, to reduce their commitment because others have entered the field.

In addition to this, the two examples allow us to offer some concluding observations that apply to both and which seem to allow for generalization.

The first, that acts as a framework for the others, concerns the double connection between what happens *in proximity*, i.e. within the system of proximity we consider, and what happens on a larger scale, when we act *for proximity*.

Actions in proximity are those of actors who, being a part of the system of proximity, are also close to each other (in both a functional and relational sense); all of the projects conceived and developed in NoLo are an example of this. And the same is true for those on which the via Cenni community was formed and regenerates itself.

Actions for proximity, on the other hand, are those that intervene on a broader system, that includes the system of proximity considered. In other words, they are actions that operate on the environment of the system of proximity. In the case of NoLo, this means all of the projects relating to technical and social infrastructure, such as the reorganization of the street system and the creation of slow mobility paths, that affect the entire city, or that of care services, that led to the creation of the WeMi spaces. In the case of via Cenni, it is the creation of a foundation that deals with collaborative living and defines rules and procedures to apply in the various interventions.

Both cases show us, over the long term, that there is a dual relationship between actions in proximity and for proximity (in the sense that there cannot be one without the other). But they also tell us that, between the two, there is not perfect symmetry. In fact, while initiatives in proximity can take place, and be successful, even without contemporary framework interventions (i.e. without actions for proximity from the outside), the opposite is not true: there cannot be interventions for proximity that are not simultaneously also interventions in proximity; or better, they can exist, but they are destined to fail.[32]

The entire history of social innovation makes this evident: new ideas are born in proximity, and if they are social innovations, they reorganize the system to which they refer by acting from the inside (this is what, in speaking of infrastructure, has been defined as self-infrastructuring). In doing so, they change the rules of the game, and thus those who propose them can find themselves on the margins or outside of current practice (and sometimes, outside of current laws). An example is people who began to transform abandoned urban spaces into community gardens, doing so without asking permisssion; those who participated in "critical mass" events (bicycle gatherings that, thanks to the strength of their numbers, occupy the streets and slow down traffic) anticipated the idea that there can be a city built for human beings, not cars, and did so as a protest action. In NoLo, those who first put tables on the sidewalk to have neighborhood breakfasts did not wait for the regulations, that came later and made it possible to use the street for this type of initiative.

On the other hand, all of the initiatives born from below, and thus that are self-organized, tell us that, in order to last in time, they must reach a form of normality. This implies, among other things, that they must encounter some farsighted social actor that operates on a larger scale and helps create a more favorable environment for them. This actor (usually a public entity, but it may also be a third sector organization or an enterprise that has adopted an approach consistent with the idea of social economy and proximity), by recognizing the social, environmental, and economic value of what that group of social innovators has done, and is driving forward despite the difficulties, uses the competences, resources, and power it has to support them and make sure that analogous initiatives can easily be born, replicated, and last in time.

We see how social innovation has its first and most evident trajectory that starts from the activity in proximity of a community, to come to interventions for proximity, and on the communities that populate it.

What cannot successfully happen, however, is the opposite process: it is not possible for a public entity, a third sector organization, or an enterprise that aims to operate in an economy of proximity, to intervene for proximity without there simultaneously being a community of place that takes part in the initiative, perceiving it as its *own* project. It should be said, though, that a path that allows for overcoming this difficulty exists. It is that which leads to acting simultaneously *for* proximity, creating a context suited to the initiative to be supported, and *in* proximity, collaborating on the construction of an ad hoc community. The mode of action defined and implemented by FHS is a clear example of that possibility: to launch its social housing plan based on collaborative living, FHS accompanied the worksites in which the buildings are built, with the sites in which the conditions are created for the birth – and then the life – of the community of residents.

Similarly, in order for the city of proximity to become a practicable program, it is necessary for those who promote it on an urban scale (i.e. the city administration) to also operate in proximity, neighborhood by neighborhood, to create favorable conditions for the growth of communities that must be protagonists on the local level. It is precisely for this reason, the need for the urban-scale program and the proximity program to proceed on parallel tracks, that its implementation cannot but take place neighborhood by neighborhood, and for subsequent experimentations, each having its own particular features (such as in Barcelona with the Superilles, as we saw in Example 2).

4.8   Community, proximity, projects

Another concluding observation regards the characteristics of the communities that are formed. NoLo shows us the community of place as a result of a web of projects. Via Cenni adds that the community exists in time thanks to a series of projects that allow it to continuously readapt. In both cases, what emerges are open and capable communities, characterized by variable geometry, that have a quasi-fractal character.

They are *open and capable* because they must welcome all of those who bring useful contributions to the project: from the experts to the designers (who are then the "design experts"), from the representatives of the public entity to those of the non-profit and private enterprises willing to contribute to the creation of a social economy of proximity.

These communities are characterized by *variable geometry* because, depending on the times and phases of the project, they require different contributions and adapt to the turnover of participants who, in time, can have more or less energy and resources to make available (and more or less interest in doing so).

They are *quasi-fractal*[33] communities because they construct projects that contain other projects (and thus other communities); and by combining with other analogous communities, they give rise to communities and projects on a larger scale. They are quasi-fractal because, despite being, at every scale, project-based communities, the characteristics of these projects (and thus of the communities linked to them) are very different at different scales. In other words, at all scales a project-based approach is required, but in each of them this project-based approach takes on a different meaning and is achieved by adopting different methods and tools.

It follows that the projects on which these communities are based are very different; they are not based on a single rationality and do not take place in a single command center (that knows everything and decides everything). At the same time, though, they are not totally independent: some shared ideas act as attractors, and there is a social infrastructure that provides support, and with the affordance that distinguishes it, favors convergence.

Finally, a third concluding observation regards the very nature of designing in complexity. The cases considered, and all of the experience in the field of social innovation, bring us to what the culture of complexity had already told us some time ago:[34] to recognize complexity, and to operate within it without seeking to reduce it and without being overwhelmed by it, it is necessary to cultivate our project-based abilities, developing them in a reflective and dialogical manner. We must know that our contribution can be significant, although never decisive; that what we do is always a co-generation that involves a maze of webs and social actors; that we must have ideas and propose them, but it is also necessary to listen, and sometimes, change our mind. Lastly, we must know that our actions can be incisive to the extent we are able to collaborate with others.

Box 4.1   Designing in complexity

In modernity, it was believed that, given a project on which to operate (a city, a neighborhood, a service, or a product), a person, designer, or project team had the ability to change it however it wanted. This is because it was thought that the designer could have all of the information and all of the power necessary to exactly define what to obtain and how to obtain it. In dealing with contemporary society it has become clear that this is not the case (and that, in reality, it was never the case): a city, a neighborhood, a social service, or an enterprise are unavoidably complex systems. Each of them is the result of a maze of interactions, that can never be fully known and controlled. Therefore, in the modernist sense of the term, they are not designable systems.

On the one hand, a careful observation of reality tells us that this non-designability in a modernist sense corresponds however to the pervasiveness of project-based activities that we find at all levels and at all scales of society: widespread project-based approaches, in which both experts and non-experts participate, and from which new sociotechnical systems and new social forms emerge. Recognizing that these systems and these social forms are the result of the joint action (that can be conflictual or collaborative) of various actors (human actors and non-human agents) means recognizing that we cannot know and control the final outcome of what we do, because what we do is only a contribution to a more general generative process, a sort of de facto co-designing in which multiple interacting entities participate.[35] By recognizing this, we acknowledge the limits of our project, our not being at the center of everything, and our not being omniscient and omnipotent. This is the first step towards a non-anthropocentric project-based approach, capable of operating in complexity.

In dealing with complexity, another necessary update regards what is designed. Today we notice that the center of attention has shifted from material artifacts to interactions (whose nature defines the quality and architecture of the system on which we would like to intervene). This change in the center of interests can be found in every area of intervention, but it is very clear when what we would like is a change of sociotechnical systems in which the social dimension is particularly important; and that, as in the cases discussed in this book, appear to us as webs of interaction, and thus encounters, conversations, and communities.

In other words, if we imagined the project as a navigation, we should think of how to do it with a sailboat, more than a motorboat. The motorboat has a motor that we think we can guide by ourselves, following a route that aims straight to where we have decided to go (or, at least, this is our illusion, until the motor breaks, or we run out of gas, or a too big wave sinks us). Sailing, on the other hand, is declaredly the result of a co-generation: it is done by us, the boat, the wind, and the currents. We need to know the boat well, listen to the wind and the current, and adapt the route to them, changing it based on need. Sailing is an exercise of continuous recognition of complexity. This does not mean being overcome by it. Sailing does not mean going adrift: rather, it means having a destination, having imagined a route taking into account the foreseeable currents and winds, and then knowing how to adapt from time to time based on what actually happens, locally. Every project, at every scale, is like this today; but projects for proximity and in proximity, for communities and in communities, are more so than others.

Notes

[1] Manzini, *Design, When Everybody Designs*, cit.

[2] Eric Klinenberg, *Palaces for the People: How Social Infrastructure Can Help Fight Inequality, Polarization, and the Decline of Civic Life*, New York, Crown, 2018 (Italian trans. *Costruzioni per le persone. Come le infrastrutture sociali possono aiutare a combattere le disuguaglianze, la polarizzazione sociale e il declino del senso civico*, Milan, Ledizioni, 2019).

[3] The term *infrastructuring* was introduced years ago by Leigh Star and subsequently revived by Pelle Ehn and her school at the University of Malmö. Susan L. Star, Karen Ruhleder, "Steps toward an Ecology of Infrastructure: Design and Access for Large Information Spaces," *Information System Research*, 7, 1996, pp. 111-134; Susan L. Star, Geoffrey C. Bowker, "How to Infrastructure," in L.A. Lievrouw, S.L. Livingstone (eds.), *The Handbook of New Media*, London, Sage, 2006, pp. 151-162; Ehn Pelle, "Participation in Design Things," Participatory Design Conference Proceedings, September 30 – October 4, 2008, Bloomington, Indiana.

[4] Greenfield, "Practices of the Minimum Viable Utopia," cit.

[5] Manzini, Thorpe, "Weaving People and Places," cit.

[6] James Jerome Gibson, *The Ecological Approach to Visual Perception*, Boston, Houghton Mifflin, 1979 (Italian trans. *Un approccio ecologico alla percezione visiva*, Sesto San Giovanni, Mimesis, 2014).

[7] Donald A. Norman, *The Psychology of Everyday Things*, New York, Basic Books, 1988 (Italian trans. *La caffettiera del masochista*, Florence, Giunti, 2014).

[8] Arena, Iaione, *L'età della condivisione*, cit. For the first "regulation," that was implemented in Bologna, see *Regolamento di collaborazione tra cittadini e amministrazione per la cura e la rigenerazione dei beni comuni urbani*, available online on the site of the City of Bologna, www.comune.bologna.it.

[9] Dimitris Papadopoulos, *Experimental Practice. Technoscience, Alterontologies, and More-than-Social Movements*, Durham, Duke University Press, 2018 (cited by Salvini, "Le ecologie che curano," cit.).

[10] When this does not happen, these project-based communities tend to become closed, identitarian groups, with all of the fragility and involutional risks that this entails.

[11] Due to their generative capacity, these products can be seen as enzymes, microscopic entities that have the possibility to activate processes on a much greater scale. The evaluation of these enzymatic projects thus should not take place considering the physical dimensions, but the transformative capacity, i.e. the effect they produce in the system in which they are introduced.

[12] The notion of "relational object" is very similar but does not coincide with that of "boundary object" introduced by Susan Leigh Star and James R. Griesemer, "Institutional Ecology, 'Translations' and Boundary Objects: Amateurs and Professionals in Berkeley's Museum of Vertebrate Zoology, 1907-1939," *Social Studies of Science*, 19(3), 1989, pp. 387-420.

[13] Obviously, it is very different if the social conversation to which we refer takes place between dozens of people, who, wanting to create a cohousing project, must reach a shared idea of collaborative living and co-designing of spaces and services to make common; or if the theme is the emergence of an idea of city that is shared by millions of people and orients multiple projects with different scales and natures.

[14] In the case of relational objects, practicability is not essential; their aim is in fact to initiate the conversation, not to make it find a direction.

[15] Manzini, *Design, When Everybody Designs*, cit.

[16] Ezio Manzini, "The Scenario of the Multi-Local Society," in J. Chapman, N. Gant, *Designers, Visionaries and Other Stories*, London, Earthscan, 2007.

[17] Daniele Cologna, "Abitare a ridosso di una storica via d'accesso a Milan," in *Esperienze e paesaggi dell'abitare. Itinerari nella regione urbana milanese*, a cura di AIM (Associazione Interessi Metropolitani), Milan, Abitare Segesta, 2006.

[18] Pietro L. Verga, "Rhetoric in the Representation of a Multi-Ethnic Neighbourhood: The Case of Via Padova, Milan," *Antipode*, 48(4), 2016, pp. 1080-1101.

[19] https://it-it.facebook.com/groups/NoLoDistrict/

[20] Cristina Pasqualini, *Vicini e connessi. Rapporto sulle Social Street a Milano*, Milan, Fondazione Giangiacomo Feltrinelli, 2018; Cristina Pasqualini, Fabio Introini, "Per un buon vicinato: la presenza "attiva" e "rigenerativa" delle social street nei quartieri di Milan," in *Costellazione Milano*, Milan, Fondazione Giangiacomo Feltrinelli, 2020; Maria Gerosa, Alessandro Tartari, "Il quartiere NoLo, un caso di rebranding dal basso: tra creatività, innovazione sociale e criticità," ivi; Erika Lazzarini, "La periferia nella città che cambia. Tra identità in definizione spinte a trasformarsi," in Francesca Cognetti, Daniela Gambino, Jacopo Lareno Faccini, *Periferie del cambiamento. Traiettorie di rigenerazione tra marginalità e innovazione a Milan*, Macerata, Quodlibet, 2020.

[21] Carolina Pacchi, *Iniziative dal basso e trasformazioni urbane. L'attivismo civico di fronte alle dinamiche di governance locale*, Milan, Bruno Mondadori, 2020.

[22] Davide Fassi, "Events and the City: When Arnold Meets NoLo," in *In the Neighbourhood*, edited by Davide Fassi and Barbara Camocini, Milan, Franco Angeli, 2017.

[23] Davide Fassi, "Quartieri come incubatori di progettualità di spazi e servizi: il caso NoLo," in Davide Crippa, *#regeneration*, Santarcangelo di Romagna, Maggioli Editore, 2020.

[24] Ezio Manzini, "Designing Coalitions: Design for Social Forms in a Fluid World," *Strategic Design Research Journal*, 10(2), pp. 187-193, May-August 2017.

[25] In 2008, in Italy, an important social housing fund was created, named FIA (Fondo Investimenti per l'Abitare). The fund's endowment is 2.028 billion euros, one billion of which was subscribed by the state bank for local authorities, the *Cassa Depositi e Prestiti*, 140 million by the Ministry of Infrastructure and Transport, and 888 million by private banking and insurance groups and pension funds. This social housing program aims to offer dwellings, services, and tools, primarily through price-controlled leases. There have been 27 local funds approved throughout the territory of Italy, for a total of approximately 220 projects, 14,800 social houses, and 6,500 beds in temporary and student residences.

[26] https://www.fondazionecariplo.it/it/progetti/servizi/housing-sociale/housing-sociale.html

[27] http://www.fhs.it/progetti/residenze/cenni-di-cambiamento/

[28] https://maremilano.org/

[29] Giordana Ferri, *Starting up communities. Un design-kit per l'abitare collettivo. Strumenti per l'housing sociale*, Milan, Bruno Mondadori, 2016; Ead., "I valori dell'housing collaborativo nel social housing: scalare l'impatto," in L. Rogel, M. Corubolo, C. Gambarana, E. Omegna, *Cohousing l'arte di vivere insieme*, Milan, Altreconomie, 2018; G. Ferri, L. Pacucci, *Progettare housing sociale: promemoria per chi progetta*, Milan, Bruno Mondadori, 2015; G. Ferri, L. Pogliani, C. Rizzica, "Towards a Sociable Way of Living. Innovating Affordable Housing in Italy," in G. Van Bortel, V. Gruis, J. Nieuwenhuijzen, B. Pluijmers, *Affordable Housing Governance and Finance in Europe: Innovations, New Partnerships and Comparative Perspectives*, London, Routledge, 2019, pp. 59-86; http://www.fhs.it/

[30] Manzini, *Politiche del quotidiano*, cit.

[31] Arena, Iaione, *L'età della condivisione*, cit.

[32] Here I consider as successful trajectories those in which, as in the cases presented, social innovation has evolved maintaining the substance of the social and environmental values with which it was born. Clearly, this category does not include those innovations which had success, even enormous success, by losing those values or even entering into open conflict with them (many cases of the current "platform economy" are a good example. See the contribution of Ivana Pais in this book).

[33] A fractal is a geometric object with internal homothety; its form repeats in the same way on different scales, thus by expanding any of its parts a figure similar to the original is obtained.

[34] Morin, *The Method*, cit.; Kagan, *Art and Sustainability*, cit.; Manzini, Tassinari, "Designing Down to Earth," cit.

[35] Latour, *The Politics of Nature*, cit.; Idem, *Down to Earth*, cit.; Manzini, Tassinari, "Designing Down to Earth," cit.

Proximate Future.
Cities of Proximity and Digital Platforms

by *Ivana Pais*[*]

There are ideas that arrive – or are rediscovered – at the right time; keywords that are able to summarize complex concepts and drive action; slogans at times ambiguous, that for this exact reason speak to different people.

The "15-minute city" is the idea that – more than others – is aggregating individuals, organizations, and institutions around a shared vision of a desirable future in the pandemic society. The lockdown and remote working have made us rediscover the importance of neighbors and services of proximity. The expression works well: it combines space and time and constructs an idea of the city starting from each citizen's steps. But as often happens with slogans, in this case the efficacy of the communication does not correspond to an equivalent clarity of the concept. This requires analyses that allow for going from suggestion to interpretation and design. This is the aim of this book, that symbolically marks a passage, with the shift from the "15-minute city" to the "city of livable proximity."

In the pages above, proximity has been analyzed in its various declinations, including "hybrid proximity" in which the opportunities for encounters in the physical world are sustained by interactions in the digital world. This proximity, as has been said, is made possible by technology, but cannot be sustained by technology alone.

My aim in this contribution is to enter into a dialogue with that proposal, starting from the question I have worked on in recent years, that is increasingly relevant in all of our daily lives: digital platforms. Throughout the text there are frequent references to platforms understood in a

[*] Full Professor of Economic Sociology at the Economics Faculty of the Università Cattolica del Sacro Cuore (Milan, Italy) and Director of TRAILab, Transformative Actions Interdisciplinary Laboratory.

broad sense, as an enabling ecosystem; in this reflection, however, I will take an in-depth look at digital platforms. I will go by stages, starting with a definition of digital platform, to then introduce platforms for livable proximity and return to two questions raised in the book: what are the relational properties of proximity platforms? And what is the relationship between urban platforms and local governance?

The examples and cases reported in this chapter come largely from the empirical research that I have carried out in recent years: while mainly based in Italy, they have a more general value, also because similar cases can be identified in different countries.

Defining the concept of digital platform

As we have seen with reference to the 15-minute city, sometimes the success of an idea depends, among other things, on choices of terminology. This is true for platforms are well: as illustrated well by Tarleton Gillespie,[1] the word platform represents an idea specific enough to mean something, but at the same time vague enough to adapt to multiple contexts and different audiences. The concept can be traced to four semantic territories: the computational meaning, that is directly linked to the idea of an infrastructure that supports the design and use of applications, also by third parties; the architectural meaning, as a "raised floor" on which people and objects can rest (railway platform, oil platform, etc.), that is connected directly to the etymology of the French *plate-forme*; the figurative meaning, as the basis on which to construct new actions, opportunities, and acquisitions; and the political meaning, that again takes its cue from the stage on which a candidate presents their positions. Digital platforms emerge evoking all of these meanings without adopting any specifically, but all have in common the idea of enabling and elevating those who use them.

Digital platforms are *metaphors*, *symbols* that possess performative power because they create imagination and in particular contribute to constructing images of the future. The reorganization of cultural processes around platforms is a process that goes in two directions: platforms transform imagination and cultural practices simultaneously give form to the institutional dimensions of the platforms. Stories about the future help mobilize resources and coordinate projects. Thus they are important not so much for their ability to realize the hoped-for scenarios, but because conceptualizations of the future orient the actions of social actors in the present.

Platforms are also *infrastructures* and thus represent the modern equivalent of railways, telephones, and services for the production and distribution of electricity in the past centuries. They are *digital* infrastructures, and thus (re-)programmable, consisting of the convergence of different systems, protocols, and networks, that enable interactions between different social actors, organized through the systematic collection, algorithmic processing, circulation, and sale of data. Platforms are potentially able to transform every form of human interaction into data, with the risk of commodification of spheres of individual life that until now had been excluded from any logic of quantification.

Platforms can also be analyzed as *institutions*, regulatory structures, because they act as private regulators in moderating online interactions. They can govern the actions of the users of platforms through their own "infrastructural power" that manifests itself in its most extreme form in the disconnection of users from the platform itself or also through the "algorithmic power" to evaluate users based on prior behavior, often through reputational mechanisms. Thus they are "evaluative infrastructures" that decentralize control despite maintaining centralized power in the hands of the platform. In this role, platforms are taking on governance capabilities that were traditionally attributed to the state, professions, and communities.

Lastly, platforms are *forms of social organization* that are differentiated from traditional forms: market, hierarchy, and networks.[2] Economic literature defines platforms as bilateral or multilateral *markets*: in reality, platforms can create markets, in which operators and users exchange goods and services, but exercise additional functions beyond simple *matching*; some even argue that they are anti-markets because they are oriented towards the construction of monopolies. If they are not markets, they are not *hierarchies* either. They certainly have a hierarchical core because they are businesses (from a legal standpoint as well), so they function based on a hierarchy – even if it is flat – but most of the functions are exercised outside of these confines, by actors who are not employees of the company. The distinctive aspect is precisely that they are able to co-opt members outside of the hierarchy (producers and consumers) and have them perform functions (such as evaluation) that are traditionally assigned to the managers. Finally, they are not networks, either. While networks are based on relationships of trust and collaboration built over time, platforms enable transactions that are often occasional between producers and consumers. The only relationship that the platform intends to maintain in the long term is that with the consumer, but this depends on monopolistic strategies and the consumer often does not have any alternative. Platforms thus have original and distinctive characteristics; they do not combine the three traditional forms, but in a certain sense upend them. They are the new form of social organization of the 21st century.

Digital platforms operate in different sectors and can take on different configurations:[3] industrial platforms (such as MindSphere by Siemens or Predix by General Electric), cloud platforms (Amazon Web Services, Salesforce), product/service platforms (Spotify, Zipcar, or Zoom), advertising platforms (Facebook or Google) and "lean" platforms, based on capital owned by users (such as Airbnb or BlaBlaCar) or the encounter between supply and demand for work (such as Upwork or Amazon Mechanical Turk). Platform companies were born mainly in the United States, but have spread globally. The most significant exception regards China, where in recent years numerous platforms have emerged that, despite being limited to the domestic market, reach significant volumes. China's BAT companies (Baidu, Alibaba, and Tencent) today compete directly with the GAFAM companies from the United States (Google, Amazon, Facebook, Apple, and Microsoft). At the end of 2020, the listed companies with the greatest value in the world were platforms: Apple, Microsoft, Amazon, Alphabet, Alibaba Group, Facebook, and Tencent. Just ten years ago, the top positions were occupied by oil companies (ExxonMobil and PetroChina). In this framework, Europe is excluded from the competition for achieving technological sovereignty, with the risk that the position of European industry in many sectors can be endangered, creating a position of economic and cultural dependency on the part of countries in the Old Continent. In addressing this question, we often assume that Europe has to enter the field of competition among the large American and Chinese platforms, adapting to rules of the game that are already defined. It would be more interesting, though, to reflect on the possibility to propose new models of platforms, that can function based on logics and mechanisms more attentive to the relationship of these organizations with local territories.

For our reflection, more than platforms as objects, it is interesting to study *platformization*, i.e. the penetration of the infrastructures, economic processes, and regulatory frameworks of platforms into various economic sectors and spheres of life. The process has led to identifying a *platform economy*, a *platform capitalism*, and at an even more general level, a *platform society*. As for industrial society and web society, platform society is also not defined in these terms based on the simple recognition of the quantitative spread of platforms, but because their pervasiveness has an impact on public and private life. In the next paragraph we will see what role platforms of proximity can play in a context of the *platform city*.

Platforms of livable proximity and questions of governance

Digital platforms as an organizational form assume a specific declination when they refer to the city of livable proximity, that can take on two principal forms: the presence of platforms intentionally oriented to strengthening relations of proximity and the use of platforms (of all kinds) by the residents of a territory.

As regards the first point, in Italy more than platforms dedicated to neighborhood relations (such as Nextdoor[4]), success has been achieved by Facebook groups dedicated to a limited territorial area (a neighborhood or town). These are dedicated digital spaces on social media platforms, that – compared to neighborhood WhatsApp groups or similar groups – are characterized by their open and public nature. The most significant experience is certainly that of the *social streets*, launched on via Fondazza in Bologna (Italy) in September 2013 with a closed group on Facebook created to bring together people residing on the same street or in the surrounding area. Social streets have been defined as "anonymous streets that become social."[5] The most interesting aspect is that social links go in the opposite direction compared to what usually takes place: while people generally meet offline and then stay in contact through social media, social streets allow for an initial digital contact between individuals, who despite living close do not know each other, and this generally is followed by personal encounters that at times lead to developing common projects. Social streets can thus help transform neighbors into a community. According to the estimates of the Observatory on Social Streets, approximately 50 percent of the people enrolled in a social street meet their neighbors offline and 25 percent go from the virtual link to what has been defined as the "virtuous" link of collaboration for a common goal, often the care for local common goods. In December 2020, it was estimated that more than 450 social streets were active – with different degrees of participation – in Italy and abroad. This is a significant number and certainly a very important experience, also because it shows the sterility of the contrast between physical links and digital links and the potential of hybrid proximity.

However, these initiatives of intentional sociality mediated by digital, are joined – much more frequently – by daily experiences of interaction through other types of platforms (for the purchase of food, for mobility, for the exchange of objects, etc.), that can become (or not become) vehicles for new forms of interaction and relations of proximity.

Localization is often ingrained in the service offered by the platforms, and proximity is the necessary condition for their functioning. In this area, the difference resides in the relational potential of platforms that act by nature at the hyper-local level, despite often being governed at the global level. The possibility to establish roots of the digital infrastructure in this case – although it may seem like a paradox – passes through physical places, that allow for moving from the scenario of "everything at/from home" in the direction of "everything close." Coworking spaces, community hubs, neighborhood concierges,[6] and even kiosks and newsstands[7] are places that enable our "onlife" relations, to use a neologism proposed by Luciano Floridi. They are open spaces, often able to involve a broad and diversified number of actors. A particularly important question is also how modes of dealing with social exclusion can represent one of the most serious risks of an urban dynamic based on infrastructure of digital platforms, and not only due to the problems linked to material access to the web or instrumental literacy, but also because of the differences in the ability to appropriate and symbolically manipulate new languages, that risk producing traditional forms of social stratification.[8]

These places are also precious because they are "points of connection" of the platforms; they correspond to points or switches of rail infrastructure, and like the point in which two tracks meet, they allow for a change in direction. Outside of the metaphor, they represent the point of encounter and exchange between communities that use different platforms. Thus, for example, a coworking space can be a physical meeting point for the users of a platform like WeMi (the shared welfare system with the participation of the City of Milan,[9] for which we refer to section 3.7 of this book, and in particular Example 6) and at the same time a distribution center for local buying groups, while the contamination between these experiences produces new local collective goods.

This aspect represents an important occasion for urban platforms that are typically circumscribed and vertical, and raises the question of the possibility to enhance such hybridizations, including through intentional forms. Moreover, initiatives of coordination at the territorial level have so far been limited to prototypes, developed principally in residential settings.

These experiences shed light on the centrality of figures who enable and facilitate relations between platform users, who go by the various names of community manager, district manager, or social delegates. An example is UpTown in Milan, a new neighborhood with more than 9 million square feet of regulated residences, social housing, and market-rate residences, that will be completed in 2022. The initiatives to construct communities were launched before the first stone was laid: in piazza Cascina Merlata, events were organized that in 2019 alone involved more than 18,000 people, that were free and open to the local area. Those who buy homes there obtain access to an ecosystem of neighborhood services, with the entire catalogue of the technological and social innovation of recent years in an app: coworking, electric car sharing, bike sharing, home delivery services, as well as physical infrastructure such as a zero-mile farmers' market, an outpatient clinic, volunteer center, neighborhood information point, tax assistance center, and personal services and commercial activities. The district manager of EuroMilano, a real estate and urban promotion and development company controlled by UpTown, plays a role that in a certain sense is analogous to that of the neighborhood social administrator and adopts methods of facilitation that are coherent with consolidated practice and competences in the third sector. In this case, the approach has been driven by a logic of commercial value growth (the value of the apartments has grown by 40 percent in two years) but it is interesting due to its implications in terms of social and territorial impact.

The connecting role that in these experiences is performed by private actors could be carried out by the local administration, which introduces a question of method that regards the governance of the city of proximity in general. A proposal oriented towards the provision of services of proximity, that allow for constructing new economic and social connections, cannot avoid a rethinking of the modes of coordination between actors, social groups, and institutions, that goes beyond the level of regulation. This request also emerges from the most recent forms of mobilization at the urban level.

The collective protest actions in regard to neoliberal policies and the experiments in social innovation in recent years have led to the emergence of a movement that has been defined as the *new municipalism*,[10] because it is the heir of movements that invoke the democratic autonomy of municipalities in political and economic life with respect to the nation-state, and that has a current dedicated precisely to the "new platform municipalism." This is a form of activism that places itself in a broader trend toward the rediscovery of the local as an area from which to start to begin forms of social transformation.

The new municipalism

The new municipalism is based on the historical precedents of municipal socialism and international municipalism, but compared to these movements that defined themselves as apolitical or anti-political, it takes on a more expressly political and "counter-hegemonic" connotation, oriented towards radical reformism, in imagining new institutional forms that incorporate an urban, non-state logic. Neo-municipalism challenges capitalism regulated at the national level and renounces claims for rights in regard to the state in favor of the construction of new forms of self-organization, able to respond to citizens' needs at the local level. More than a relationship of complementarity/substitution with the state, the interesting aspect of the new municipalism in our view is that it assumes as a constituent trait the project of a "politics of proximity"[11] that goes beyond simple physical closeness and does not imply a fetishism for the local, referring to closer and smaller problems, and in which proximity is the interest towards "forces that unite," opposed to the politics of "forces that separate." The birth of this new municipalism is symbolically traced to the Fearless Cities summit organized in June 2017 in Barcelona, and it is important to note that, in addition to the 700 participants from 180 cities and 40 countries, on that occasion representatives of 100 platforms were present, confirming the emergence of platforms as a new form of civic action.

The new municipalism takes on different spirits, including that of "new platform municipalism" as an alternative to platform capitalism, through mobilization of civil society to establish new civic platforms.

The movement also distances itself from the discussion on the smart city, oriented exclusively to the issue of technologies, which it counters with forms of reorganization of the coordination between urban infrastructure, work, mobility, and governance in ways that allow for reterritorializing the space and reconfiguring citizenship.
The new municipalism aims to democratize urban platforms and use the platforms in broader projects of economic and urban democratization.

This attention to digital platforms on the part of new civic movements also implies taking a position with respect to their implications, with particular reference to two questions amply addressed in the book, but that have important specificities when declined with respect to digital platforms of proximity: the relational properties of platforms and the relationship between urban platforms and local governance.

The relational (but not only) dimension of digital platforms

In April 2016, Mauro Covacich published an article in *La Lettura* of the *Corriere della Sera* newspaper entitled "Today I remained silent." The writer told of an entire day spent without ever interacting with other people: he withdrew money from an ATM, paid for his shopping at the automatic check-out, worked out at the gym, had lunch at a self-service restaurant, traveled from Rome to Milan and back, went to the movies; all without ever opening his mouth. And he commented: "Life is never here, it is never now. Displaced, deferred, far in space and time from the point in which we are breathing, it is a life always lived elsewhere, a practice whose anticipated execution will take place down there, at the end of the workout or the trip or the day, or – and this is no different – it is already taking place at every moment, constantly, in the parallel universe of the web."

The web, social networks, internet of things, artificial intelligence: digital allows for obtaining goods and services without any interaction with the people who are close to us, and at the same time, for communicating in real-time with people who are far away. But let's try to change the perspective: what would happen if we used the same technology to construct and nourish relationships of proximity?

Digital allows us to work out in the gym following the instructions of an avatar, without even greeting those who are pedaling next to us, or it can put us in contact with unknown people who live – or pass through – our neighborhood to organize a basketball game. Technology allows us to reserve a ticket on the *Frecciarossa* fast train paying a supplement for the silence area or to share a trip with BlaBlaCar. We can make a movie reservation online and enter the theater by scanning a QR code or search on ComeHome[12] for a cultural event organized at the home of a friend.

Technologies are not neutral: they can be designed to favor relations or eliminate them, to centralize power or distribute it, to recognize individual contributions or extract value from them.

The debate on digital platforms emerged precisely from a sensitivity to the relational dimension. We can recognize this, once again, from the terms used: we only began using the concept of platform a few years ago; initially we spoke of the *sharing economy*.

The sharing economy

The sharing economy was born as a response to needs created by the economic and financial crisis of 2008 and with reference to the three dimensions of sustainability: economic, through the exploitation of scarce and underutilized resources and the reduction of transaction costs; social, through the expansion of individual and collective social capital and the return to the rooting of economic exchange in social relations; and environmental, with the connection with forms of circular economy, through the increase in the use of durable goods, the recycling of products, and the sharing of productive assets.

Experiences that had emerged spontaneously and independently found themselves converging under the umbrella concept of "sharing economy": from barter platforms or home exchange, to crowdfunding and time banks, to the point of de facto including all digital platforms for the exchange of goods and services. This created problems of definition, but shed light on common elements among very different practices – regarding values or organization – prevalently inspired by the logic of production and peer-to-peer consumption, summarized by Michel Bauwens:[13] anti-credentialism or equipotentiality, i.e. the absence of an a priori selection of those who will participate in the project or exchange; holoptism, i.e. the participants having access to all of the available information; organizational decentralization; and the already-cited attention to sustainability in its various forms. In the most advanced experiences, or at least as an ideal reference, more was added to these characteristics: participatory governance; the adoption of fair economic models and remuneration systems; the choice of open and transparent technologies in data management; the importance attributed to social inclusion and the reduction of discrimination; and the assumption of responsibility with respect to negative impacts.

The digital sharing economy thus presents itself as a hybrid form between reciprocity and market, or better, as an expansion of reciprocity in the direction of the market. In collaboration, the cycle of reciprocity becomes "short," that is, we expect restitution quickly, and as similar as possible to what was given. The more instrumental motivations prevail over intrinsic ones, the closer we come to the model of cautious reciprocity, in which the parties do not intend to enter into a relationship that obligates them beyond the contingent interest that moves them to cooperate. Collaboration is thus similar to market transactions, even though the relationships of production or consumption of the exchanged goods are such as to require an agreement between the parties that cannot be defined a priori as a "complete" contract. So some knowledge, although superficial, and a certain degree of trust in the partner are necessary. However, unlike strong reciprocity, the initial precautions, the predominantly extrinsic motivations, and the contingency of the relationship do not allow for cementing social links that give rise to specific interpersonal trust. This is rather derived or indirect: it depends on the ability of the institutional context in which the collaboration takes place to circulate reliable indicators of reputation. In launching a collaboration, people cannot count on the direct experience of prior relationships, and must trust the judgment of others, who have recognized the reliability of a partner in the past. Subsequently, the learning made possible by the collaboration launched allows those same people to in turn generate reputation in a cumulative process that can become self-sustaining. In order to this to happen, though, it is necessary for the institutional context of collaboration spread by the platform to have the trust of the participants.[14]

This is not the place to discuss it, but the reconstruction of the transformations of the concept of sharing economy can be useful for those who approach the proposal of the city of proximity. Born as a counterculture, in open criticism of neoliberalism and as a proposal for a "different economy," it then gained the approval of the marketing departments of companies that offered models distant from any logic of sharing to legitimize the spread of their business model. Russel Belk[15] has defined them as "pseudosharing" platforms, in contrast to true sharing based on forms of collaborative consumption that create collective identification and forms of reciprocity. This process has cast a shadow on the practices of the sharing economy, with an impact on producers and consumers who have lost the ideal, value-based push that had motivated their participation until that point.

A decade after the emergence of these practices, the three forms of economic, social, and environmental sustainability have taken different paths. On the one hand, we have global platforms oriented towards economic sustainability, born principally in Silicon Valley, that construct an alliance between owners of the platforms and venture capitalists willing to inject patient capital, while waiting for the platform to reach a monopoly. In view of this goal, the platform makes incentives available to consumers who thus benefit from efficient and low-cost goods and services, but also find themselves linked (often involuntarily) in an alliance with platforms and investors that harms workers. On the other hand, we have initiatives of small dimensions, with stronger social, environmental, and ethical roots, but that often have problems of economic sustainability.

The platforms that place a focus on the relational dimension can be traced to three categories: platforms for the access to underutilized goods offered by private individuals, platforms for collaborative consumption, and platforms for the quasi-equivalent exchange of goods and services. Each of these categories can be declined originally in the perspective of the city of proximity.

Access to underutilized goods owned by private citizens – from a room in a private home to a ride in a car – is the area in which collaborative models, based on peer-to-peer exchange and logics of reciprocity, have most often given way to digital market platforms. The most evident example is that of hospitality: platforms that seek to combine long-range connections with the promotion of local territories and characteristics. Among the pioneering experiences is this area is Couchsurfing, a platform based on indirect reciprocity, without payment, that lost users just in the years Airbnb was expanding. In its initial years, Airbnb itself largely exchanged paid hospitality among private users, but has now principally become a commercial marketplace where the offers are represented by private agencies. The weakening of the relational dimension is favoring the emergence of experiences that aim to revive this component: these are ethical platforms that intend to reintroduce attention not only to the regularity of the rental contract (also from a tax standpoint) but the authenticity of the relationship between host and guest, and – an aspect that is particularly interesting for our purposes – to the repercussions of these practices on local territories.

An interesting case is Fairbnb,[16] a platform created in 2016 as a "non extractive alternative to the current vacation rental platforms." Initially born as a movement in Venice, Amsterdam, and Bologna, at the end of 2018 it registered legally as a cooperative. In the Fairbnb Manifesto we read: "Websites that offer short-term vacation rentals allow for affordable and unique travel experiences. Locals can supplement their income while sharing their culture. But this model can come at a cost, driving up real estate prices, fragmenting communities, and closing local businesses. Across dozens of cities, technology-driven tourism is making it harder for locals to live in and manage their own neighborhoods." The platform aims to allow "hosts and guests to connect for meaningful travel and cultural exchange, while minimizing the cost to communities." It does this, first of all, by reinvesting the profits in social projects at the local level. The platform is still in the startup phase and there are criticalities in implementation, but the model proposed highlights a sensitivity to social roots, at the local level, of the exchanges that take place through it.

The second area is *collaborative consumption*: platforms that organize buying groups from local producers, crowdfunding platforms, and platforms for organizing events among private individuals. Among the most interesting experiences in a dimension of proximity are those developed in the context of food buying: from alternative food networks, that use digital infrastructure to more efficiently organize activities and are strictly rooted in a dimension of proximity, to platforms that continue to leverage environmental sustainability and food quality (such as *la Ruche qui dit Oui!*[17]), but in which payment for the service reduces the tasks attributed to the consumers, and at the same time, the need for relations between them.

This category also includes crowdfunding, that we can define as the accumulation of small investments in single projects by a large number of individuals (the crowd) through digital platforms.[18] The sector is particularly interesting because it sees the coexistence of large global platforms with other platforms that are national, regional (Ginger[19] for Emilia-Romagna) and local (which we will return to in the next section) having a good user basin. An exemplary case is the equity crowdfunding campaign organized by Forno Brisa[20] of Bologna, a company with a team of 32 young people having an average age of 29, that to expand its bakery activities in February 2020 collected 1.2 million euros from 379 people.

The spread of platforms for the organization of events between private individuals is also interesting. An example is the already-cited Come-Home, that allows anyone to organize an event at their house (a dinner, a theatrical performance, a yoga lesson) and allows the users of the platform to participate. This makes temporary aggregations possible around moments of entertainment that can also lead to the construction of locally-rooted communities of interest.[21]

The last category is the *quasi-equivalent exchange of goods and services*: barter platforms (like Freecycle[22]), time banks, complementary currencies, and so on. These are interactions that go beyond the exchange of equivalents, because the link between the parties takes on value. These platforms spread widely in the years after the 2008 crisis precisely due to their ability to combine instrumental and expressive motivations: saving or the access to goods/services otherwise not available, and at the same time, the facilitation of new interactions and relations. Sardex,[23] a company founded in Serramanna, Sardinia in 2009, defines itself as "an integrated platform designed to facilitate relations between economic actors operating in a given territory, and to provide them parallel and complementary instruments of payment and credit" (at the end of 2020, over 10,000 companies registered in various Italian regions had made available the equivalent of 200 million euros per year in goods and services to exchange with complementary currency inside the company's network, and their employees receive part of their salaries in Sardex credits). The studies carried out demonstrate that mechanisms of this type strengthen the circulation of money and at the same time the construction of bonds of trust at the local level.

To summarize, the relational dimension that was at the center of the first sharing platforms is now less present in the global platforms, that are more oriented towards market exchanges. For precisely this reason, a counter-movement is emerging oriented towards the promotion of relational platforms, that are also ethical and democratic, and have strong local roots, often converging on physical places, as we will see in the next section.

Urban platforms and local roots

Although they are present in rural contexts or internal areas, platforms are born and develop principally in cities, for various reasons. First of all, because in order to function they require density. This is true especially for platforms that facilitate the encounter between supply and demand for online services, but then require physical meetings. For example: platforms for the home delivery of food cannot operate if there is too much geographic distance between the restaurant and the customer. But the city as a stage or theater of platform capitalism is only the first level. What interests us most here is the fact that platforms change the way people experience cities and reconfigure urban spaces, especially in the passage of scale to proximity. Platforms construct cities.[24] But cities are also the place where the social problems they generate become most strongly evident: the gentrification driven by Airbnb, the risks for health and lack of labor protections for riders, and the bankruptcy of local shops substituted by Amazon are only some of the signs in this direction.

The spread of platforms has led to the shift from services managed by local companies, often regulated by the public administration, to services managed by multinational corporations, whose offices are concentrated in a few cities at the global level. Passenger transport companies such as Uber or Lyft, for example, have their headquarters, but also their secondary offices, in only 29 cities around the world.[25] This contributes to strengthening the trend towards "world-cities," i.e. cities in which the global flows of capital and people are concentrated, a direction from which Italian urban centers have so far remained excluded. European cities and those in Italy must therefore deal with platforms that mainly have their offices abroad.

This is not the only limit, though: the city is the level most exposed to the risk of social changes, but at the same time, also that with fewer levers for intervention, in terms of capacity for taxation, development of an industrial policy, or spending ability. And since at lower scales (whatever the perimeter deemed pertinent) it becomes even more difficult to use these elements, we see that cities are called on to identify new modes of intervention.

Moving within the limits described, the strategies adopted by cities in regard to platforms can be traced to three types of actions: regulate, support, and create/adopt. Regulation is the most traditional form, and has been implemented above all in the area of mobility and tourism/hospitality to reduce the impact of gentrification. However, from the prospect of the city of proximity, it is more useful to reflect on the two other forms: support and adoption.

Support for the platforms has been exemplified well by the case of *Consegne Ethiche* (Ethical Delivery) in Bologna, a cooperative platform for home delivery promoted by the City of Bologna, in collaboration with two local cooperatives (*Dynamo* and *Idee in Movimento*), that has operated since October 2020. Among the points of the Ethical Delivery Manifesto, in addition to respect for worker rights and protections, we read: give value to territorial service; keep the relationship between merchants and customers alive; and facilitate processes of solidarity in the city. The goal is thus to create communities of place and start from the interactions channeled through the platform.

Local administrations generally support ethical platforms through three channels. The first regards consulting based on skills within the administration. In the case of *Consegne Etiche*, the city administration has made two people available to the project from the *Fondazione per l'Innovazione Urbana* (Foundation for Urban Innovation) to support the design and startup phase. The second is as a "user" of the platform, in the role as the client. Fourteen percent of GDP of the European Union and ten percent of Italian GDP is spent through public procurement.[26] The introduction of evaluation criteria that give careful consideration to the relational, ethical, and democratic dimensions can provide platforms a particularly useful volume of jobs, especially in the startup phase of the process. This is what is happening in the case of *Consegne Etiche*, with the home delivery of books from public libraries. The third, and perhaps most important channel, regards reputational capital: the public administration, through registers or other methods, can recognize the platforms that respond to criteria of social justice. In the case of Bologna, the promotion of *Consegne Etiche* followed the drafting of a *Charter of Fundamental Rights of Digital Work in the Urban Context* in May 2018, that – not coincidentally – was signed by only two local platforms (Sgnam and MyMenu).

In the case of Consegne Etiche, the city administration made itself available to a specific project also using its own communications channels. One of the limits of local platforms is in fact the difficulty of reaching the network effects that are characteristic of platforms. While global platforms use risk capital to *scale out*, disseminating their projects on a broader territorial scale, or to *scale up*, changing institutions at the level of policies, rules, and laws, for territorial platforms the goal is to *scale deep*, with an impact on values and convictions. The legitimization offered by institutional recognition, together with the use of institutional communications channels, that reach a broader number of citizens, can represent an essential contribution in this direction, activating and contaminating already-existing local communities rather than creating new ones.

Sharing cities

Support for ethical platforms by numerous local administrations has led to the formalization of a network of 42 Sharing Cities, that at the Barcelona Summit of November 2018 signed a Joint Declaration. The Declaration consists of ten principles, that we can summarize as follows:

1. differentiation between the different models of digital platforms with particular attention to collaborative models;
2. labor: possibility to increase income through new agreements relating to work and fiscality;
3. labor: fair benefits and protection of workers' rights;
4. inclusion: access to work and prevention of any form of discrimination;
5. public protection: respect for health and safety standards;
6. environmental sustainability: sustainable use of resources within the framework of the circular economy;
7. data sovereignty and citizens' digital rights: implementation of technological sovereignty policy and digital ethical standards, adopting an approach to data as a common good;
8. city sovereignty: guarantee respect for the legal jurisdiction of cities;
9. economic promotion: development of local collaborative economic ecosystems;
10. general interest to preserve the right to the city and "urban commons."

The signing of this Declaration represents an important step, first of all because, at the moment in which various urban platforms are taking on specific configurations in different urban contexts, it reaffirms some common principles that are shared at the international level. In addition, the Declaration enters into the merits of the various implications and takes a position on single questions, within the limits of the power of action of urban government. This is an interesting operation, because it revives the visions that inspired the emergence of collaborative economic practices and declines them in the area of effectiveness of urban governance and represents a useful base for the further passage from the level of the city to that of proximity, that is still absent in these reflections.

The third strategy to orient the choices of urban platforms by local administrations is the creation of new platforms or the adoption and personalization of existing platforms. This strategy is adopted by administrations that intend to use the platforms as modes of organizational innovation. Civic platforms are not generally limited to automating pre-existing processes, but create digital structures to support new strategies of participatory governance.

As the sharing economy aims to expand the sphere of reciprocity, contaminating it with the sphere of the market, at the same time what Christian Iaione and Sheila Foster have defined as the *co-city*[27] expands the logics of reciprocity in the direction of redistribution. This form consists of a link of reciprocity between people who share a sense of belonging and distinguishes the community structures, including communities of place. The social link is established not so much horizontally through the consolidation and spread of "I-you" moral relations, as for strong reciprocity, as vertically in recognizing each of ourselves in a "we" from which obligations derive towards all of the members of the community. This form, based on shared values and rules, can thus spontaneously regulate the access to and use of common goods, i.e. goods that are often rivals in consumption but cannot be excluded given their essentiality for the life of communities and the individuals who are a part of them. This allows us to differentiate the trust that characterizes this form also from the reputational form typical of sharing structures. Indeed, in this case it is trust that is generated by the investment in the community and establishes moral obligations in regard to all of its members (that are more or less binding). Reputational trust, on the other hand, despite being indirect and generalizable, is based only on information concerning prior behavior, but leaves the actors morally free to exit the relationship despite paying a cost in terms of future reputation. However, although generalized, this form of reciprocity is not universal, since it is defined by the perimeter of the community itself. Unlike traditional forms of redistribution of public goods, in the hybrid forms of sharing of common goods, the links, although in a light and transitory form, are foundational for the modes of exchange.[28]

An example of this mode is *civic crowdfunding*, that is, the use of crowdfunding for the realization of projects that strengthen the dynamics of community at the local level and produce common goods. It can be defined as a new model of financing and co-design in which various actors (citizens, associations, businesses, foundations, and other entities) collect economic resources to promote various types of urban projects. It is one of the possible tools, supported by digital technologies, that allows citizens to construct visions of the future and design cities, services, and urban spaces through local initiatives from the bottom up.

There are various elements of potential of this new form of collaboration between active citizens and public administrations. First of all, civic crowdfunding can allow administrations to interface with the community in a direct, simple, and transparent way, involving actors with whom they do not have other occasions for interaction and identifying through this channel unsatisfied needs and emerging social problems. Moreover, civic crowdfunding can promote innovative forms of public-private partnership. Lastly, thanks to this new tool, citizens have the possibility to show forms of innovative activation, that are "lighter" than the forms of traditional civic participation, but precisely for this reason, are potentially more inclusive.

The case of the City of Milan's civic crowdfunding is particularly significant because, in the 2020/2021 edition, the administration explicitly tied the civic crowdfunding to neighborhood projects: it selected twenty initiatives presented by non-profit groups in the area and offered a grant of up to 60,000 euros to the projects able to reach at least 40 percent of their resources through donations from citizens. In December 2020, seven projects had reached the goal, collecting 85,000 euros from 1,200 donors, and seven other projects were launching their own campaigns. These include new places of proximity: the Lab Barona-Repair Café, that defines itself as "a special place, in which, between a cup of tea and a coffee, objects for the home are exchanged, repaired, and transformed, and new friendships are born, for people of all ages!"; or the CineMarmocchi in the Giambellino neighborhood, with small armchairs and child-sized furniture, that aims to develop "a culture of proximity that is able to dialogue with the territory," and thus states: "we will look for our collaborators in the neighborhood and the movies will be in their original language with subtitles in order to be accessible to residents, who come from every part of the world."

The analysis of the results of the previous edition of the City of Milan's civic crowdfunding, held in 2016, allows for reflecting on the impacts of these practices. The first question posed regards the ability of that tool to expand participation and the possibilities of local democracy. Some authors highlight the limits of these processes: the funders have only the choice of supporting the project or not, while more detailed, and perhaps more promising, forms of participation are only present in cases where local actors are offered the possibility to participate in the revision of the project, to modify it, enrich it, and redesign it based on their expectations, needs, and competences. In the experience of Milan, this has happened more frequently downstream of the funding campaign, when some promoters have more directly involved the funders and local communities in the phases of implementation of the project.

Another important question regards the digital divide. A criticism that is directed at these experiences is that they are able to bring benefits to a small minority of the population, already self-selected and capable of making use of a broad range of tools. Moreover, it is thought that the better organized groups, with strategic and design capabilities, generally come from privileged social (and urban) contexts. Yet in the case of Milan, the City's decision clearly favored the insertion into the process of projects located in marginal areas or those with social disadvantages, or aimed at fragile populations, thus orienting the processes in the direction of a reduction of inequality, although through small, often niche projects.

A third aspect regards the suggestion that civic crowdfunding, like many bottom-up initiatives promoted by civil society, associations, or private individuals, risks contributing to a reduction of the presence and projects of local administrations in many areas previously covered by local welfare. This trend is due to budget scarcity, that in this view, could somehow be exacerbated by the presence of a very active local society, that could gradually replace the public entity. On this point as well, the case of Milan tells us something different: the mechanism of preselection of the projects and the subsequent co-financing seem rather to guarantee a presence of the City both in the strategic phase and in the phase of feasibility of the projects, and thus to assist the consolidation of new forms of public-private partnerships not only with the large structured actors of the third sector, but also with smaller, diffused actors.[29]

Proximate future: platforms as new "local collective goods"?

In declining the proximate future as a future of proximity, in addition to platforms for the exchange of goods and services, an unexpected role is being played by platforms for communication and sharing of information and knowledge, that in the pandemic period have supported the passage to remote work and distance learning, and that now seem destined to alter the relationship between territory, economy, and society.[30]

Remote working is – at least potentially – the most incisive lever of social transformation for the coming years, and what can lead to the configuration of a city of proximity that affects every sphere of individual and collective life. From the standpoint of businesses, the relevant territory has always played a role in the choice of location: the resources available at the local level favor companies that decide to operate in a certain territory, and at the same time, the presence of those companies can represent an element of attractiveness for other resources. In this sense, the literature on local development has proposed the concept of "local collective goods for competitiveness"[31] precisely to indicate the goods and services made available in the context of a specific territorial situation. They are invisible factors linked to geographic proximity, with which drivers of development are associated, including the success of small and medium-sized enterprises that otherwise would not be competitive, not having the resources to internalize those goods/services or to acquire them on the market. The offer of those goods is assured through forms of local governance.

With the strengthening of distributed work, two questions are posed: the first regards the processes of reorganization of the production of, and access to, local collective goods; the second the emergence of new local collective goods.

As regards the first point, the recourse to forms of distributed work could change the geography of the areas with a service vocation, leading to the abandonment of buildings used for service functions, similar to what has happened in the past few decades for buildings in industrial areas. At the same time, new forms of territorial reaggregation could emerge. This has an impact not only in terms of urban regeneration of the abandoned areas, but with respect to the processes of exchange of information and knowledge necessary from a perspective of economic innovation, even if it is only incremental. In the most competitive local economics (with the various definitions of industrial districts, learning regions, smart regions, and *milieux innovateurs*) some of the most important local collective goods for competitiveness are linked to the training of human resources and processes of research and development. If the workers do not necessarily reside in the same territory in which the company has its offices, how do the dynamics of localization of the places assigned to training and research change (in particular, professional training centers and universities)? How is it possible to recreate that virtuous circle between centers of elaboration and spread of knowledge and businesses that characterizes in particular the most innovative local economies (to look outside of Italy, think of Silicon Valley)?

The response to these questions can come not only from the reorganization of the processes of production of local collective goods as a response to the impact of the new digital platforms on the economy and society, but from the analysis of the digital platforms understood directly as local collective goods. The presence of an ecosystem of digital platforms integrated and rooted in the territory in fact represents a resource available to the people, companies, and organizations who inhabit it, and can support the emergence of new economies that are nourished by new forms of proximity.

To give an example, think of the potential of local platforms for the management of data. Data have been defined by the Economist as "this century's oil." Unlike natural resources, data must be produced and processed. Moreover, they are not fungible the way money is. For precisely this reason, it is hard for them to be exchanged on the market, and despite expectations of this sort, it is difficult to construct models that allow for redistributing (monetary) value to those who have supplied their data. At the same time, data can have an enormous informational value for the communities able to process them. In other words, data can represent new local collective goods. This is why some are investigating the possibility to construct local platforms, that can also be tied to existing organizations which citizens can trust, for the storage, aggregation, and above all interrogation of data in order to create value for the relevant communities. The data made available by the single individual (from health data to data on mobility), once aggregated at the territorial level, and if appropriately interrogated, can generate information that represents a value for the communities themselves.

If the keyword to analyze local development in the last century was competitiveness, now collaborative models seem to be emerging strongly. It is not only about enabling networks between businesses (local collaboration to face global competition), but constructing economic models that are rooted locally and connected globally, in which the exchange of resources can follow the hybrid logics of expansion of reciprocity in the direction of the market and the redistribution that we have analyzed above. In this sense, digital platforms can represent "local collective goods for collaboration," together with other physical and digital infrastructure:

from broadband connections to the presence of spaces, and in particular collaborative spaces that allow for connecting short networks of economic and relational roots with long networks of exploration of new ideas, information, and knowledge.

Retracing the experiences and reflections presented in the pages above, it is evident that the city of proximity thus also passes through the design of forms of local rooting of digital platforms and assemblies of digital technologies, physical places, individual uses, entrepreneurial logics, and forms of civic activism. Until now, we have observed what has been produced as an equilibrium between the forces that have emerged in the various fields, with territorial ties principally at the city level. The proposal of the "city of livable proximity," as it has been developed in this book, implies a passage to a lower level, which makes a project-based effort necessary in the direction of a desirable future.

Notes

[1] Tarleton Gillespie, "The Politics of 'Platforms'," *New media & society*, 12(3), 2010, pp. 347-364.

[2] For further discussion of these reflections, we refer to David Stark, Ivana Pais, "Algorithmic Management in the Platform Economy," *Sociologica*, 3, 2020.

[3] Nick Srnicek, *Platform Capitalism*, Cambridge (UK)-Malden (MA), Polity, 2017 (Italian trans. *Capitalismo digitale. Google, Facebook, Amazon e la nuova economia del web*, Rome, LUISS University Press, 2017).

[4] https://it.nextdoor.com/

[5] For further discussion of social streets, the experiences promoted and the motivations of the participants, we refer to the publications of the Observatory on Social Streets of the Catholic University of the Sacred Heart, and in particular to Cristina Pasqualini, *Vicini e connessi. Rapporto sulle Social Street a Milano*, Milan, Fondazione Feltrinelli, 2018 (available at https://fondazionefeltirnelli.it/).

[6] For more: Monica Bernardi, "Portinerie di quartiere: innovazione sociale tra digitale e locale," in Giampaolo Nuvolati (ed.), *Enciclopedia Sociologica dei Luoghi*, Milan, Ledizioni, 2019, pp. 335-351.

[7] See the interesting French experience of *Lulu dans ma rue* https://www.lulu-dansmarue.org/

[8] For an in-depth analysis of the passage from spaces to places, see the interesting book by Paolo Venturi, Flaviano Zandonai, *Dove. La dimensione di luogo che ricompone impresa e società*, Milan, Egea, 2019.

[9] https://wemi.comune.milano.it/

[10] For further discussion of the questions addressed in this section, see Matthew Thompson, "What's so new about New Municipalism?" *Progress in Human Geography*, 2020.

[11] Bertie Russell, "Beyond the Local Trap: New Municipalism and the Rise of the Fearless Cities," *Antipode*, 51(3), 2019, pp. 989-1010.

[12] https://comehome.fun/

[13] Michel Bauwens, "The Political Economy of Peer Production," *CTheory*, January 12, 2005.

[14] For further analysis, see: Ivana Pais, Giancarlo Provasi, "Sharing economy: A step towards the re-embeddedness of the economy?" *Stato e mercato*, 35(3), 2015, pp. 347-378.

[15] Russell Belk, "Sharing versus Pseudo-Sharing in Web 2.0," *The Anthropologist*, 18(1), 2014, pp. 7-23.

[16] https://fairbnb.coop/

[17] https://alvearechedicesi.it/it

[18] For more, see Ivana Pais, Paola Peretti, Chiara Spinelli, *Crowdfunding. La via collaborativa all'imprenditorialità*, Milan, Egea, 2018.

[19] https://www.ideaginger.it/

[20] https://mamacrowd.com/project/forno-brisa

[21] For an analysis of the new economic communities that are formed through digital, we refer to the brilliant work of reconnaissance and analysis performed by Marta Mainieri, *Community Economy. Persone che rivoluzionano imprese e mercati*, Milan, Egea, 2020.

[22] https://www.swapush.com/

[23] https://www.sardex.net/il-circuito/

[24] Sarah Barns (in *Platform Urbanism. Negotiating Platform Ecosystema in Connected Cities*, London, Palgrave, 2020) writes: "Quaint distinctions between the 'built' and the 'digital' are collapsing, just as software makers are literally becoming 'city builders'" (p. 15).

[25] Shauna Brail, "Unicorns, Platforms, and Global Cities. The economic geography of ride-hailing," in M. Hodson, J. Kasmire, A. McMeekin, J.G. Stehlin, *Urban Platforms and the Future City: Transformations in Infrastructure, Governance, Knowledge and Everyday Life*, London-New York, Routledge, 2020, pp. 53-69.

[26] *Comunicazione della Commissione al Parlamento europeo, al Consiglio, al Comitato economico e sociale europeo e al Comitato delle regioni. Appalti pubblici efficaci in Europa e per l'Europa*, Strasbourg, October 3, 2017 (available at https://ec.europa.eu/).

[27] Sheila R. Foster, Christian Iaione, "The city as a commons," *Yale Law & Policy Review*, 34, 2015, p. 281.

[28] For further analysis, we again refer to Pais, Provasi, "Sharing economy," cit.

[29] This analysis is drawn from Carolina Pacchi, Ivana Pais, "Il crowdfunding civico tra reti, comunità e ruolo del governo locale," in Fondazione Ambrosianeum (eds.), *Una metropoli per innovare, crescere, sognare*, Milan, Franco Angeli, 2017, pp. 117-134, to which we refer for further analysis.

[30] The reflections that follow have been in part proposed in Ivana Pais, "Smart-working e nuovi spazi di lavoro: come cambiano i beni collettivi locali," *Menabò di Etica ed Economia*, 136, 2020.

[31] For a presentation of the relevant debate, we refer to Colin Crouch, Patrick Le Gales, Carlo Trigilia, Helmut Voelzkow, *I sistemi di produzione locale in Europa*, Bologna, Il Mulino, 2004.

www.ingramcontent.com/pod-product-compliance
Lightning Source LLC
Chambersburg PA
CBHW051742250726
48659CB00001B/202